Alert the Media

Alert the Media

How the American Indian
Movement used the Mass Media

Marilyn Catherine McDonald MA

2010

Dedication

This book is dedicated to the memory of my thesis advisor
Dr. Robert Fulford
Creative and Communication Arts Department
University of Portland in Oregon.

CONTENTS

Truth,
whether in or out of fashion, is the measure of knowledge,
and the business of the understanding;
whatsoever is beside that,
however authorized by consent, or recommended by rarity,
is nothing but ignorance, or something worse.
John Locke (1632-1704)

ACKNOWLEDGEMENTS

Author's note: "A Study of the Interrelationship between the American Indian Movement (AIM) and the Mass Media" was the original title attributed to my masters' thesis in 1977. The new title "Alert the Media" emerged later to reflect an advertising and public relations slang expression for getting the message out and gaining attention or awareness for a product, person or issue. And, in keeping with the times, the terms "Native American" and "Indian" are used interchangeably.

Special thanks, and the book's dedication, go to the late Dr. Robert Fulford, Professor in Creative and Communications Department at the University of Portland in Oregon, who encouraged me every step of the way. I wrote the text he always wanted for his "Philosophies of Communication" course.

The chapter on "Movement Toward Social Change" was written with guidance from Dr. James Stemler, Professor in Sociology at the University of Portland.

Dayton O. Hyde's book, *The Last Free Man: The True Story Behind the Massacre of Shoshone Mike and His Band of Indians in 1911*, (although not included as a resource in this study) sparked my interest in the American Indian.

Katharine McCanna, Book Counselor, patiently listened to the details of this research and pointed out the publication possibilities.

A word of appreciation for Devere East Man "Papasan" who said I wouldn't have the nerve to write the things he told me.

Marilyn Catherine McDonald MA

An expression of gratitude goes to my family for their patient indulgence with my passion for learning and writing.

PREFACE

The longevity, effectiveness or ultimate survival of twentieth and twenty-first century mass movements toward social change depend, almost entirely, on their interaction with and treatment by the mass media.

Marshall McLuhan, social-cultural theorist, speaks with considerable authority on the link between media and movement in *The Medium is the Massage*:

> "Societies have always been shaped more by the nature of the media by which men communicate than by the content of the communication.... It is impossible to understand social and cultural changes without knowledge of the workings of media."[1]

The intense interaction between the mass media and mass movements has generated undercurrents of public discontent and dissatisfaction with the media. Radio, network and cable television, magazine, newspaper, and now, Internet news reporting are criticized by public figures and private citizens alike. The media's perceived participation in and encouragement of undesirable activities and repetition of messages connected with the increasing number of political and social causes and movements polarizes the public.

The bulk of this study attempts to unravel the relationship between a particular political movement seeking social change, the American Indian Movement (AIM), and the mass media of that time. AIM, a major movement that trailed after the Civil Rights and anti-Vietnam War movements, began in 1968 and extended its overt activities through 1976, until its influence diminished and its ability to command media attention faded.

In 1976 the Subcommittee to Investigate the Administration of the Internal Security Act and Other Internal Security Laws labeled AIM as "revolutionary" based on testimony by Douglass Durham, an FBI operative who worked his way into an administrative position in AIM. His involvement lasted nearly two years.

Indian communities were sharply divided regarding their affiliation with AIM, or their dissatisfaction with the movement and its methods. Other Indians, on and off the reservations, were only vaguely aware of a movement taking place.

AIM's spectacular and sometimes militaristic activities prompted considerable media coverage. The controversy surrounding AIM caused many people to react, almost immediately, in a way that was either favorable or unfavorable to the movement.

The purpose of this study is to explore as many facets of the movement and its interaction with the media as possible, within the context of the times in which much of the activity occurred. Considerable effort was exerted in keeping the information balanced, neutral and factual. The luxury of hindsight was unavailable.

A literature search in advance of topic selection indicated that this would be a challenging and ambitious pursuit of resources. There was not a single book available, at that time, dealing specifically with the American Indian

Movement, and only a few periodical articles focusing on the interrelationship between AIM and the media. There was a strong feeling expressed by professors involved in the areas of sociology and communications that such a study, with the accompanying list of sources, would prove to be a valuable research tool for other scholars. Conversations with book distributors indicated a keen interest in the results of such a study. Also, my personal interest in learning more about the American Indian culture and relating that information to the mass movement expanded my research and final manuscript to more than 150 pages.

The study upon which this book is based required thorough research into several academic disciplines. Its interdisciplinary approach touches on sociological, psychological, philosophical, historical, theological, anthropological and speech communication areas, with emphasis on journalism.

The thesis chapters were arranged in such a way as to provide readers with as much background as possible before reaching the actual relationship between AIM and the mass media. AIM may have suddenly appeared on the front pages of newspapers across the country, but that first appearance was one event, a result of a continuing process that started long before the formation of AIM.

Chapter I – Introduction discusses the terms "mass movement" and "mass media." It also discusses an individual's passage from event to event in a continuing process, from one culture to another. The chapter presents a profile of a Sioux Native American spiritual leader the Portland, Oregon. Since much of the thesis focuses on the Sioux influence and involvement in AIM activity it seemed fitting to presents the thoughts of one Sioux Indian who had personally committed himself to the ideology of the American Indian Movement to the point of helping in the formation of an AIM chapter in the Portland area.

Chapter II – Movement toward Social Change is a necessary definitive study of movement terminology. Without an understanding of the general nature of a movement it would be difficult to understand how AIM and other movements came to be. This chapter defines the basis of motivation leading to the formation of a recognizable political movement. The chapter examines how social conditions precipitate discontent, and how individuals perceive the need for change. It discusses the ways in which people join forces, set goals based on their generalized beliefs, acquire leaders, and maintain membership. Strategies and confrontation with authority also are examined.

Political movements require resources in order to self-perpetuate. One of the major resources considered by leaders and members of modern day movements is the use of the mass media channels of communication.

Chapter III – Mass Media's Power and Responsibility examines the potential for media to inform and influence. Mass media channels of communication have passed through phases of development and become considerably sophisticated and complex. Along with the increased potential for delivering news and information to great numbers of people has come an increased responsibility for giving the reader, viewer or listener an accurate interpretation of the events and processes being reported. Mass movement leaders in the twentieth and twenty-first centuries have become increasingly aware of the mass media as a political tool, a major resource for presenting their message to their publics and applying pressure on authorities. AIM leaders developed a high degree of media awareness and planned their activities to attract media attention. AIM used the media, and the media allowed themselves to be exploited until many of the media representatives realized they were becoming part of the movement process.

Chapter IV – Native American (Indian) Culture provides background for the motivations behind AIM by exploring aspects of the culture – the language, beliefs, customs and institutions. It is necessary to define the Indian oral culture and dependence on symbolism to understand why the AIM leaders found it necessary to return to the reservations to study their own culture and recapture their heritage. Many of them grew up in the cities and lacked the channels of communication necessary for attracting new members. Their need to speak a common language prompted a renewed interest in their tribal philosophies and religious rites.

This chapter details many of those perceptions and symbolisms. The study of the Ghost Dance is particularly important as it relates to AIM's 1973 occupation of Wounded Knee, South Dakota. Although the mass media misperceived much of the significance concerning the event it is not surprising considering the amount of research necessary to relate two events – the massacre of 300 Indians at Wounded Knee in 1890 and the occupation by AIM in 1993.

The information regarding re-institutionalization is pertinent to the study of AIM. It places the movement within a context of power and leadership and also in conflict with other organizations and institutions – some of them Native American based.

Chapter V—The American Indian Movement (AIM) deals more specifically with the formation, leadership and goals of AIM. Information is presented to demonstrate the manner in which AIM came to depend on a media image. Attention from the mass media was, in fact, one of AIM's major goals. AIM was patterning much of its activity after previous mass movements. How mass movements gained attention served as a preliminary guide in planning and executing major events.

Chapter VI—Wounded Knee in 1973 is concerned with how and why leaders and movement participants entered and occupied Wounded Knee in 1973. The chapter concerns itself with the role of the government in precipitating the confrontation, and the role of the media in covering and reporting the event. AIM capitalized on whatever it could to gain media attention, especially at Wounded Knee. The Wounded Knee event caused media representatives to take a closer look at their manners and methods of covering and reporting news.

Chapter VII—Douglass Frank Durham, FBI Operative examines AIM from the perspective of the man who rose high in the ranks of the movement and probably helped to plan and execute several of AIM's activities because of his many and varied skills. Parts of his testimony before the Senate Subcommittee investigating internal security were selected and included in this chapter. Many of the remarks and reports of events are concerned with AIM's use of the media.

Chapter VIII—Dennis Banks in Oregon focuses on the leader's activities in avoiding extradition to South Dakota. The chapter allows newspaper headlines to tell the Dennis Banks story of court involvement. By this time, 1976 and 1977, AIM is fading from media attention. Does the movement continue, though not publicized? That question will be answered in Part Two, AIM and Mass Media after 1977.

Chapter IX—Conclusion states that the mass movement has the appearance of being dead as the visible part of the organization is weakened and public attention diminishes. Why did AIM diminish? Or did it? The Conclusion briefly discusses, chapter by chapter, the academic, professional and public communications benefit of this study.

I
INTRODUCTION

The terms "mass movement" and "mass media" have gained acceptance in their related disciplines. The terms are used throughout this study to denote great numbers of people being involved in the transmitting and receiving of messages, and great numbers of people performing along the same course toward common goals. The terms are used with the understanding that individuals create movements, and individuals send and receive messages. The movement, in effect creates a common language.

A common language holds a nation or a movement together. It has been historically demonstrated that a nation's conqueror must break down the common denominator for new philosophies and new ways to take hold. Learning new symbols, new language, separates individuals from their past culture and causes disorientation.

The passage from event to event within that phase of disorientation is the story of a continuing process. The nature of that continuing process makes news coverage, at its best, less than adequate. And every good reporter knows and feels the agony of what might have been written if time and space had allowed. The responsibility of using language weighs heavily and the choice of words to convey moods and tone can be inadequate. Each person's selective perception weighs and balances each part that goes into the making of the whole. This study was weighed and balanced with that kind of precision. No piece of information went into the original thesis without weighing carefully its right to remain.

It was an unusual experience to have researched and reported along the accustomed linear western cultural patterns and at the same time to have been aware of dealing with material and persons of an oral culture. It became necessary to gain a perspective regarding these language-culture differences and similarities so that the thesis could maintain its balance.

A set of personal interviews with a Sioux Indian medicine man, who had been identified with the Portland, Oregon chapter of the American Indian Movement and its formation stages, helped put the study in proper perspective. Trying to understand one man's background and involvement increased the reality of the study. That one man was Devere East Man, respectfully called "Papasan" by Indians and by his other friends. "Papasan" means head of the house. The following is the story of one Sioux Indian.

Papasan

Devere East Man does not have a telephone. He responds to messages left for him at the Whitecloud Center, the national center for American Indian and Alaskan Native Mental Health Research and Development, where he is employed as a youth counselor. East Man also conducts Indian religious rites at Adair Village, where Indians with alcoholic problems are aided in a respiritualization and recapturing of lost pride. Our first meeting was held in a classroom of the Portland Urban Indian Center.

The big, brown-skinned Indian wore a royal blue velour long-sleeved shirt, blue jeans that cinched a well-endowed abdomen, ankle-high hiking boots, gold-wire frame eyeglasses centered on broad facial features, and long hair braided with leather strips to the ears and beaded ties from there to the ends that hung to the breast pockets of his shirt. He folded his hands, with the large knuckles and protruding wrist bones, on the desktop, closed his eyes for increased concentration, and began to speak with a slight list in a slow reflective manner.

"This is going to be a lesson for you. You won't get it in any other classroom," he began to unravel the story of the Indian as I readied my pen and steno pad, wishing I'd asked to run a tape recorder to free my attention from note taking.

"The Indian believes in the natural order of the universe." He spoke of the young men, the AIM leaders who grew up away from the circle of Indian culture and power so that they could see how a corrupt government was forced on their people. He said that only a few held on to the truths and the Indian suffered a loss of dignity and freedom by submitting to the new ways. "The missionaries came to see heathen savages, idol worshippers.... Indian people have respect for human beings. We never had welfare, insane asylums – we took care of our own."

I continued to take copious notes as Papasan spoke of the written language of the white man. "The Indian was called superstitious because he didn't have a written language. You don't have to remember if you have a written language. You can deceive with written language. The white man taught in linear language, he could burn his

3

bridges and not have to remember.... The Indian knows things far beyond what his white brother knows."

Papasan said that when the white brother came, the Indian welcomed him. The white man wanted to be free and the Indian spread a blanket for him – made a large teepee. Then more came, with fear, deceit and hate. The Indian sat down with the white man in council but the missionaries, soldiers and government were pulling the strings in back. When the meeting was over the Indian heart was sad. He held his white brother by the hand and said, "Brother, someday when you become a human being again we'll sit down.

"There have been many years of ugliness," said Papasan, "and now the people are coming back."

East Man was born on the Rosebud reservation in South Dakota in 1930, and went away to the Indian boarding school in Pierre, South Dakota, at the age of five-and-a-half. "I learned a new way. They make you a dumb servant of the system. He [the ruler] must crush me or be crushed."

The Indian spiritual man speaks disparagingly about his introduction to Christianity. "The first time I walked into a church they asked me if I wanted to be a Catholic or a Protestant. Catholic sounded pretty groovy."

East Man was prepared for his new school and his new religion. "They gave me a haircut, short pants, cloddy shoes, and I felt foolish. I had to fall on my knees before a man on a cross and a white lady holding a baby – I prayed to idols."

The white man said the Indian ways were superstitious and idolatrous, but East Man saw the new ways as idolatrous: "They make you forget the old ways. The teachers were all white – trained to break the will of the Indian." He recalled the moment he rejected Christianity, when the teacher hit him in the mouth for talking to the other Indian children in the classroom in the Indian language.

"At the age of 33, I began searching for a new way of life. The Grandfather [Great Spirit] sent me to school [into the world to learn the mysteries of life."

Papasan asked for a piece of paper and drew the Sacred Wheel. He traced a path clockwise from innocence to wisdom and back to innocence. He wrote "1890 – 1973" and underscored it four times, indicating the time of the Ghost Dancing and massacre at Wounded Knee the first time in 1890, and the second time of the Ghost Dance at the 1973 AIM occupation of Wounded Knee, South Dakota. "The circle is complete. We don't need it anymore. It will not be done again.

"Life is a circle – everything happens twice," Papasan continued his reflective manner and I felt warm and good and absorbed in what he was saying. Everything he said began to make sense and I began to forget my objectivity. "The future is our past," he continued, "and the past is our future. Summer came and summer comes again. It's a mystery."

He took a verbal slap at the white man's clocks and calendars. "The Indian never marked time, never harnessed time. He remembers events. He has a good memory. He remembers creation and how it all came to be here. We were taught as youngsters about the four ways of life. There are colors to care for the four parts of the world. All were created by the same One. The red man was always here. He was told he migrated from other lands. That's bullshit, we were always here."

East Man believes that the Indian was born in innocence and that the Christian's concept of being born in sin or darkness creates an unnecessary fear of life and the Life Giver. He criticizes the missionaries for their misuse of the cross to frighten, to make people feel guilty, to make people spiritually sick. "When he is spiritually sick it brings physical sickness. The Indian medicine man treats the whole man. The white man treats parts."

Papasan says that the Shaman [holy man] represents honesty, trust, love and generosity. He can never lie to the people because he smokes the pipe. Papasan tells the story of a holy man whose life parallels the Christian's account of the life of Jesus:

> "There were six tribes in the motherland. A boy was born without a father. Everyone knew he was to be a sacred man, a medicine man, and a holy man. When he was a young man he called the people together and told them he must go across big waters. There were people calling for his help.

> "'I'll be back. But I might have an accident. When you see blood on a certain tree [cedar] know I've had an accident. See on the tree – a cross in blood.' "The brother went east from here. The star in the sky means the brother is coming back. It means the rising of the Indian people.

"They saw the star in 1973. They gathered at Wounded Knee. They let their hair grow long again. Both red and white men were seeking and searching."

East Man says that when the Indian cut his hair he lost his culture. His culture was his strength. He can't live without his culture. The longest he can last is 200 years and then he will start to consume himself – destroy himself. There is a race of dying people on the continent trying to save themselves.

The Indian sees God in nature and nature in God, according to Papasan, and "each animal teaches us a way to live." He also speaks of protecting children from the adult world. He says that children find out too much about the adult world through television. "TV is a vacuum cleaner. It pulls out – and also puts something back that is not good. Young people build on time. Everything is fast, spiraling. There's no place for the old. The Indian family takes in all."

According to East Man the white man tried to destroy the Indian's culture by taking his religion away, by outlawing some of the religious rites. The government eventually dropped the restrictions placed on the Sun Dance. The Sun Dance is performed spontaneously at a time known to the Indians, in mid-summer. East Man says the rituals are performed by tribes located along the north to south line running through the center of North America. South Dakota, and the Sioux nation, is at the center of that line and one running east and west.

The Sun Dance is a time of self-discovery. A time of communicating with the Great Spirit. A time of fast-ing and sweat lodges. A time for piercing the flesh. "All I have to offer is my skin, my flesh, my heart." The degree of pain endured in the Sun Dance determines the degree of euphoria and religious fervor experienced. Papasan said he has pierced his pectoral muscle with the branch of a cherry tree.

Some see visions. East Man says the greatest vision is the white buffalo. He has not seen the white buffalo. (When I met him a few years later he had the vision and changed his name to White Buffalo.)

When he took part in the Sun Dance in Greengrass, South Dakota in 1976 there were two dancers who saw the white buffalo. In a vision, the buffalo changed into a person and brought the pipe. At the end of the dance there were two pipes. When sickness comes, for which there is no cure, East Man believes that the smoking of the pipe will protect the Indian.

East Man did the Sun Dance with AIM leaders Dennis Banks and Russell Means, and AIM Spiritual leader Leonard Crow Dog. Papasan says that the 1973 occupation of Wounded Knee happened because the Indian had to protect himself. "You can't negotiate with savages. They [government] only understand guns."

He accuses the white man of being narcissistic, a man in love with himself and his creations – creations that will eventually destroy him because he is so dependent on them. According to East Man, "the white world is vicious, angry, and lacking culture. 'Takes-the-fat' is the name for the white man because he picks out the best part for himself. He stole the best parts of language. He calls the

Indian incompetent, but the Indian can self-preserve and the white man can't"

———

The next time I met with Papasan we sat on the hood of a small red car in front of the Urban Indian Center and I asked him the meaning of the term "Indian Summer" for the kind of autumn day we were experiencing.

"I don't know. Maybe it's because it's beautiful." Then he began to respond to my questions about his involvement with AIM. He had co-chaired the Portland chapter with John Talley for one year after the Wounded Knee incident in 1973.

He gradually redirected his interests to Portland Community College where he took classes in sociology, English, math, and anthropology. "I was studying white people." The spiritual leader says he has a hard time talking with intellectual people. "It's all garbage and you have to break it down."

He said Wounded Knee was good because it exposed the ugliness. "It was damn good – there's so much corruption in the Bureau of Indian Affairs." He says that the people went to Wounded Knee during the conflict to bring back eyewitness reports because they couldn't trust the press. In the summer of 1975 they were going to Custer, South Dakota for a celebration and the newspapers reported that "AIM was coming fully armed to raise hell. That was bullshit," said East Man, "but the Crow police deputized people and gave them weapons. The FBI was around. We had our prayers at the battlefield and nothing happened."

When asked about the role of FBI operative Douglass Durham, he said, "I don't know what kind of man it takes to be an informer. I don't know what's in the heart. He gains the trust then informs. It's an awesome kind of game to play – dealing with the virtue of the Indian people."

He said that AIM made its point. "They reached their own people and the whole world. The publicity was good. Some was accurate. But the attitude of the government is the same." He has little hope for a change without the abolition of the Bureau of Indian Affairs. "There are 17 or 18 Indians in there for every bureaucrat. At least 70 to 80 percent of the money goes to the administration of BIA and 15 cents out of the dollar gets to the people." He said that the Indians never wanted citizenship and there is a movement seeking independence, a seat in the United Nations, and foreign aid.

But Papasan concentrates on the spiritual movement. He says he is a seeker, a hunter and a warrior, and there is no end to the mysteries as one door opens after another. He works with the alienated Indian who has sought his lost pride in alcohol – trying to teach him to like himself and not show contempt. In returning to the old ways the Indian discovers his lost identity.

———

The scholar, and the alienated Indian, both search for an identity – for a thesis statement within a mountain of research – examining a series of events as close to their context as humanly possible.

The scholar, the intruder into history, imposes a perception by selection and analysis, separating and studying the parts with the hope of eventually pulling it back together into the complete unit that existed prior to the tampering. The scholar plunges into the dark, deep water of wisdom, attempting to meet the challenge of examining without prejudice.

II
MOVEMENT TOWARD SOCIAL CHANGE

Power is control, and control is power. In a democratic society there is supposed to be a fair distribution of control and power so that the people are free to manage their own lives and resources.

Those who govern hold power. Those who maintain wealth (money, property, resources) possess power. Those who have the potential for manipulating and controlling the minds and actions of great numbers of people would be said to have awesome power.

The people who lack sufficient governing, monetary or communicating power sometimes join forces in an effort to change something that they agree can't be changed by exerting individual effort. And thus, mass movements are born.

This chapter seeks to define the general nature of the mass movement phenomenon by examining social conditions, individual perceptions and collective behavior as basis of motivation.

Marilyn Catherine McDonald MA

Basis of Motivation

The retrospective analysis of a movement sometimes reveals details responsible for propelling underlying discontent through phases of protest and into a historical mass movement. One person's theories or criteria for studying a particular collective human process can prove to be an inadequate tool and much of the study becomes educated guesswork.

Since historical events are analyzed as selective and individual perspectives it becomes increasingly important to examine mass movements within the times in which they occur. Because, it is within the tensions, problems and pressures of those times that seeds of discontent take root and grow into social movements.(1) A sociological report by Gary Marx and James Wood details some of the strains underlying collective behavior as:

> "...resulting from economic crisis, war, domination, mass migration, catastrophes, and technological change. When a group's traditional or anticipated way of life is disrupted, the likelihood of collective behavior is increased. As expectations that previously guided actions fail, pressure for change is exerted."[2]

The social conditions that provide comfort and security for some individuals may have an opposite effect on others who will experience relative deprivation, conflicts and tensions. For instance, the Vietnam War effort provided some citizens with a sense of security because they perceived it to be a control of a threat by the Communists to take over a country. On the other hand, young men eligible for the draft perceived the war as a personal threat to the outlining of a future course of action and career choices.

Discontent arises from the individual's perception of relative deprivation which is described as a "perceived discrepancy between men's value expectations and their value capabilities."[3] So that, when the social conditions increase expectations without increasing capabilities for realization, the intensity of discontent increases. In the case of the Black Power movement of the Civil Rights movement the inequities for attainment of resources and goods gradually prompted great numbers of blacks to seek change through political pressure.

Language scholars extend their analysis of motivation toward political action to the individual's prior orientation and symbol learning process. Blacks, Chicanos and American Indians who have been raised in an environment that stresses human relationships, spontaneity and verbalization through an oral culture may interpret an event differently than a suburban, white, middle-class member of society. Kenneth Burke describes motives as shorthand for meanings of situations:

> "Our introspective words for motives are rough, shorthand patterns of discrepant and conflicting stimuli.... Since we characterize a situation with reference to our general scheme of meanings, it is clear how motives, as shorthand words for situations are assigned with reference to our orientation in general..."[4]

Marilyn Catherine McDonald MA

Social psychologists advocating the symbolic interaction orientation of behavior say that individuals relate to their external environment through the use of learned symbols. They respond to symbols and mediate through the use of symbols, and language itself is symbolic.[5] Each individual develops a set of cognitions, means of acquiring knowledge, that include beliefs and attitudes regarding the nature of the world, society, other people, groups to which he belongs, and himself.[6]

Leon Festinger, a psychologist, introduced the term "cognitive dissonance" to describe a condition of "Psychological incompatibilities between two or more items of knowledge or beliefs of an individual."[7] For instance, an American Indian may perceive the earth as "Mother" and benefactor, and experience extreme discomfort or dissonance, when he sees the white man lay down hundreds and thousands of miles of asphalt and concrete for roads that allow both the white man and the Indian easier access to remote locations.

Individuals in the state of cognitive dissonance experience a critical need for establishing internal comfort and consistency. The condition itself can be a motivating factor for personal action to bring about a consistency. The individual may choose to rationalize the discomfort by ignoring or avoiding the conflict, or reduce the dissonance by changing their view of the world – or change the world to fit their view.

Anthropologist Carlos Castaneda spent ten years interviewing and attempting to acquire the knowledge to gain membership into the world of Don Juan, a sorcerer in Mexico. He said that Don Juan convinced him that the convictions he [Castaneda] held in mind as the real world were merely a description of the world:

> "A description that had been pounded into me from the moment I was born...For Don Juan, then, the reality of our day-to-day life consists of an endless flow of perceptual interpretations which we, the individuals who share a specific membership, have learned to make in common."[8]

Individuals who are bound to their description of the "real" world view certain social conditions as problematical, undesirable, and even diabolical. Their perception of the world (as it should be) is "good." They begin their assent toward perfection based on that perception. The ideas, and events and people who oppose the "good" begin to be defined in the individual's mind as "not good." An enemy is defined – and in the case of collective behavior or mass movement – a common enemy is perceptually described.[9]

When two or more people share a common view of the world, its problems, how it should be, and who is the common enemy, then discontent and a sense of purpose are mutually generated. It is a time of indecision, and the beginning of movement toward change:

> "The inception period of a movement is a time of indecision: of alienation, auscultation, and the innovation of public tensions. It is a time for the identification of destination and devils, the 'Mecca' of the movement, and the 'evil principles' it opposes....

Movements begin when some pivotal individual or group – suffering attitudes of alienation in a given social system, and drawn (consciously or unconsciously) by the impious dream of a mythic Order – enacts, gives voice to, a **No**."[10]

When a significant number of people say "No" to the system, conflict occurs and another heightened drama of life moves forward. Some rhetoricians have determined the drama of the mass movement to be essentially political because of certain major concerns with governance or domination, and the wielding and obeying of authority.[11] Participants perceive their part in this drama as essentially moral and begin to cooperate with others of like views and act in concert.

Once the participants in a social or political mass movement view their role as good, participation then requires commitment to change, toward seeking a solution to a problematic situation. That commitment to a cause, an ideology, becomes the driving force that holds the movement together as it attempts to transform, reform, redeem or offer alternatives to the society in which their particular drama takes place.[12]

Goals

In the beginning the participants in a movement are keenly aware of what they are against and who, or what, represents the common enemy. It is a time of creating doubt, indecision and division – creating a sense of guilt among those to whom the message is communicated.[13] At the beginning of the movement, it is the best time to draw other alienated people away from the system – those who empathize and identify with the image of the protestor. That image may be viewed through communications in the media or by personal associations.[14] Many of these alliances or coalitions are temporary, and seemingly, unlikely combinations of people who may be experiencing anomie, people who are encouraged by the system to strive for goals and in one way or another denied access to the means of attaining these goals.[15] People who have fallen by the wayside, stand on the sidelines, marginal, uncommitted and not caught up in significant social enterprises.[16] they may share in some, but not necessarily all, of the generalized beliefs of the protestors. Generalized beliefs typically congeal among:

1. Politically disinherited peoples, especially migrants;
2. Colonially dominated peoples;
3. Persecuted minorities;
4. In an inflexible political structure;
5. In post-revolutionary situations and;
6. In situations marked by the failure of government by political parties.[17]

As an example, participants in, and supporters of, the American Indian Movement (AIM) may share in the generalized belief that the Indian was the "caretaker of the land" before the white man came, and that the white man has perpetrated injustices by assuming ownership and division of that land to the detriment of the Native American peoples.

As a result of perceived injustices, many of the American Indians assume a political alienation posture – estrangement from the politics and government of their society, a feeling that public matters are not their affair, that government is not "their" government, that the constitution is not "their" constitution – a posture that implies rejection.[18]

Sociologist Neil Smelser has defined movements in collective behavior terms as being either norm or value oriented. Norms are concerned with specific rules of conduct and values are the desirable ends. He defines the value oriented movement as:

> "...a collective attempt to restore, protect, modify, or create values in the name of generalized belief. It involves components of action, reconstitution of values, redefinition of norms, reorganization of the motivation of individuals, and redefinition of situational facilities."[19]

A critique of the Smelser definition suggests modification of the concept of generalized belief:

> "The norm-value distinction must be supplemented by the recognition that a given movement or even a faction in the movement, can be simultaneously characterized by its desire to change norms and values..."[20]

The American Indian Ghost Dance religion that evolved in late 1800 is an example of a value oriented movement that resulted from a series of crushing defeats dealt to Native American Indian tribes and perceived by them as a disorganization of their culture and less dignity.[21]

Smelser's study indicates a series of six time-ordered conditions for collective behavior: 1) structural conduciveness; 2) strain; 3) growth and spread of generalized beliefs; 4) precipitating factors; 5) mobilization of participants for action, and: 6) breakdown of social control.[22]

A critique of Smelser's work sets aside three of the conditions (structural conduciveness, generalized beliefs, social control) as distinguishing norm-oriented from value-oriented movements. Value orientation involves less structural differentiation, emphasis on value-oriented beliefs, and the degree of influence exerted by authorities to maintain control is directed to the particular orientation. The tendency being less control over norm-oriented movements to keep them from developing into value-oriented movements.[23]

As movements progress they become subject to the same kinds of internal and external pressures that affect changes in individuals. The collective body struggles to maintain some homeostasis by reexamination of its structure, goals, and means for achieving those goals. In this context, movements have been described as "rhetorical striving, a becoming...progress from stasis to stasis; for both the origins and the objectives of a movement are motionless..."[24] Activities begin in indecision and end in decision persevered in.

Over time social movements experience crisis, and changes of their internal organizational and ideological nature – a transformation. They may shift to "more conservative goals, organization maintenance, and oligarchy... in addition they consider factional splits, increased radicalism, and relations with other social movements."[25] Individuals involved in the leadership and membership begin to interpret events within differing frameworks of reference, leading to different conclusions of what reality is.

"Shifts of interpretation result from different ways in which we group events in the because of, in spite of, and regardless of categories."[26]

Structure

There may be a variety of answers to the question of which comes first, the leader or the movement? As the movement grows from protest, riot or disturbance into a recognized ideological body with a significant number of followers the leaders may emerge or be enlisted. In either case leadership is essential.

Past studies have indicated that there are different types of leaders for different types of movements, just as there are different types of followers. One study of the Russian Revolution from 1905 to 1917 identified six role types: rebel, striker, propagandist, intelligentsia, party organizer, and upper-level politicians.[27]

A sociological study by Zurcher and Curtis suggests that in a small or emerging political movement, organizational leadership orientation, goal specificity, and incentive structure are particularly important variables. And in those movements where leadership is oriented toward goal diffuseness and solidarity incentives the following characteristics are likely to occur:

> "An expressive orientation, charisma, radical tactics, inclusive membership criteria, mergers and coalitions with other social movements, longer duration, susceptibility to pressure for organizational

maintenance, goal transformation, an emphasis on person-changing goals, and the lack of a parent organization."[28]

In the value-oriented movement, charismatic leadership is a prime characteristic. Charisma has been described I terms of the divine:

"...a certain quality of an individual personality by virtue of which he is set apart from ordinary men and treated or endowed with supernatural, superhuman or at least specifically exceptional powers and qualities. These are such as are not accessible to the ordinary person, but are regarded as of divine origin or as exemplary and on the basis of them the individual concerned is treated as a leader."[29]

Martin Luther King's charismatic leadership of the Civil Rights movement in the sixties gained a total kind of commitment from his followers. They placed their hopes in him for a collective reconstruction of their values, and with his death the movement began to die as well.

Toward the end of the twentieth century the American Indian began to resist the encroachment of the white man. They looked to Chief Sitting Bull as a spiritual charismatic leader, and with his death much of the heart went out of the Indian peoples. Followers of the American Indian Movement (AIM) believed their leaders to be endowed with exceptional qualities specific to the Indian culture, and its needs for reorganization and revitalization.

Individuals searching for heroes and heroines – role models – begin to identify with movement leaders and project themselves into the movement. They learn new conceptions of themselves, perhaps at variance with objective reality, and begin to interact symbolically with the leaders and other participants in the movement.[30] The group then serves as a frame of reference for ordering experiences and perceptions of self, and egos become bound emotionally together in relation to the demands of the group, or movement.

A modern movement may be run by professional leaders who acquire outside funding and present a false impression of the numbers of persons and purposes involved:

> "Outside funding from the government or foundations mobilizes the professional social movement, which is comprised more of leaders than of members. Leaders will often give the impression that there are many members of the movement when, in fact, 'the membership may be nonexistent or existing only on paper.'"[31]

There may be a diversity of attitudes among the rank and file, as well, and a discrepancy that exists between the beliefs of the leaders and the beliefs of the followers.[32]

These are critical points that require careful investigation and responsible reporting on the part of the media. The media attention given to a movement and its leaders can relegate an ideological process to oblivion or catapult an event into an item of national interest.

A political movement has its "in" group and its "out" group. The participants who are "in" are totally committed and actively involved in a network of communications between leaders, members, auxiliaries and the general public through the media. The "out" group may give tacit approval to the ideological process and object to the specific goals and methods of achieving objectives. The "out" group may have a genuine vested interest in the results of the mass movement but be unable to contribute their name or effort because of a risk factor. They may lose status or resources. The "out" group may be of the same ethnic persuasion and voice open objection to the actions of the "in" group but privately welcome the attention given their people.

Such diversities existed in the black communities as a result of the Black Panther movement; in the Indian communities over the American Indian Movement (AIM), and in the Mexican-American communities with the Caesar Chaves, American Farm Workers controversy and movement. In general, the "out" groups have ties, rewards and interests in the system being opposed by participants in the movement, and in many instances a state of cognitive dissonance exists, pulling them from one side to the other, until a firm decision of commitment can emerge.

The mass movement is promoted, and promotes itself, when there is a significant symbolic expression of the group as a collective; when they are treated as a group by others – including the media – when they project a common style of life, norms and values; and when there is a high rate of interaction.[33]

The degree to which a movement is "inclusive" or "exclusive" regarding membership may also determine its potential longevity. Zald and Ash predicted the growth, decay or change in a movement by citing four hypotheses. Two of them relate to membership:

> "3) Movements which aim to change individuals and employ solidarity incentives are less likely to vanish than are movements with goals aimed at changing society and employing mainly purposive incentives. 4) Inclusive organizations are more likely to fade away faster than exclusive organizations; the latter are more likely to take on new goals."[34]

If an organization or movement desires insulation by exclusive membership requirements and more internal control with the idea of changing individuals, "the less susceptible it is to pressure for organizational maintenance or general goal transformation.[35]...but exclusive organizations are more likely than inclusive organizations to be beset by schisms."[36]

The predisposition of the movement leaders toward "inclusive" or "exclusive" membership continues to be a determining factor at various junctures in the movement's history. When one goal has been reached and another is determined for pursuit the characteristics of membership become a factor:

> "If it is characterized more by inclusive than by exclusive membership:
> - The heterogeneity of the membership is greater;
> - The stress is more on societal than on individual transformation;

- The tendency is more toward group than toward individual recruitment;
- The centralization of the leadership and authority structure is less."[37]

For certain individuals, group membership becomes more than an official or physical affiliation; it becomes a symbolic matter, a spiritual commitment when they and the group are one:

"To be influenced by a group means to become involved in a network of communication through which the values and purposes of the group come to be shared.... The degree of an individual's commitment to a given group is indicated by the position he occupies in the network of communication, and by the manner and extent of the group's influence on his behavior."[38]

Methods

Methods of operation and means of achieving mass movement goals may shift according to decisions arrived at due to pressures within the movement itself, or as a result of resistance, yield, or subtle pressures from the system and society it is attempting to change. Those who are in positions of authority within that system will provide a variety of responses to the leaders and members of the mass movement and its ideology. They may attempt to satisfy certain groups and use force to put down others.

Leland Griffin's analysis of the rhetoric of movements as defined by Kenneth Burke has divided movement toward social change into two strategies. The first is designed to promote decision and convert the estranged and the second is meant to provoke to action, to create order.[39] While attempting to create order, according to the perception of the participants in the movement, militancy or violence sometimes occurs.

The national Task Force Study on Demonstrations, Protests and Group Violence, chaired by Dr. Milton S. Eisenhower, issued a report that indicated political and economic power were not as easily shared or turned over to powerless outsiders as some might imagine:

> "The admission of Indian tribes, members of labor unions, or the mass of oppressed black people to full membership in American society would have meant that existing systems would have had to be transformed, at least in part, to make room for the previously excluded, and that, in the transformation, land-hungry settlers, large corporations, or urban political machines and real estate interests would have had to give ground."[40]

The report also raised three critical points about protest and violence in America that should be kept in mind when examining mass movements:

1. One of our consultants examined every incident of protest reported in the *New York Times* and the *Washington Post* from September 16, to October 15, 1968. Of 216 incidents, thirty-five percent reportedly involved violence. Since protests resulting in violence are more likely to be reported, the actual propor-

tion of violent incidents is doubtless much
lower.

2. It is often difficult to determine who was 'responsible' for the violence. The reports of our
study teams, however, clearly suggest that
authorities bear a major responsibility. The
Kerner Commission findings reveal a similar pattern. Of the violent incidents reported
above, in only half did the violence seem to
have been initiated by the demonstrators.

3   ...a serious analysis of the connections between protest and violence cannot focus
solely on the character or culture of those
who protest the current state of American
political and social order.... The results of our
research suggests that mass protest is an out-
growth of social, economic and political conditions; that such violence as occurs is usually
not planned, but arises out of an interaction
between protesters and the reaction of authorities.[41]

Often, protesters warn authorities that if they follow a certain policy dire consequences will result. This is
not necessarily a threat, but merely an act of persuasion
if the protester lacks control over the dire things predicted.[42] Authorities may differ in their reactions to different
groups:

"There may be many reasons why authorities would
prefer to see some groups more contented than others. They may share the values and interests of one
group and prefer to satisfy them for that reason.

> Or, some may have more resources or access than others and they may relieve pressure by yielding ground to the most powerful among the potential partisans.

> The greater the inverse relation between the amount of resources controlled and the amount of discontent among potential partisans, the freer the authorities are from influence."[43]

Often, the participants in the mass movement perceive a situation in which alternative means for achieving their goals are unavailable. They do not possess the facilities for reconstituting the social situation:

> "[They] rank low in wealth, power, prestige, or access to means of communication.... [so] the aggrieved group is prevented from expressing hostility that will punish the persons or groups considered responsible for the disturbing state of affairs.... And the group cannot modify the normative structure, cannot influence those who have the power to do so."[44]

Sociologist William Gamson has defined three resource areas: inducement, constraints and persuasion. Inducement encompasses money, favor, services and opportunities. Constraints include the ability to add some new disadvantage to the situation of some specified authorities, such as threats of force, violence, and physical abuse, seizure of persons or property, or blackmail. In the area of persuasion the protesting group would hope to gain access to authorities through public opinion and the communications media, through reputation for knowledge or wisdom, and personal attraction.[45]

Large or small amounts of resources may be necessary to produce the desired degree of influence. Members of a movement may be content with newspaper publicity that increases public awareness of their existence in the community:

> "If success is judged in terms of immediate influence such claims might appear to rely on a false coin – a confusion of public attention with actual influence on policy. However, if success is judged in terms of building organizational support and tapping potential resources, the coin may be quite real."[46]

There is not a direct correlation between the amount of resources a unit possesses and the amount of influence it exercises. While the discontented group assembles all its resources to achieve its goals the forces of social control are also assembling "resources to combat the discontented group. This dual mobilization sets up the dynamics of the movement."[47]

Gamson suggests examining discontent and struggle for power from two perspectives: The influence perspective of the protesters takes the vantage point of potential partisans and attempts to influence choices of authorities. The social control perspective is held by the system authorities who attempt to achieve collective goals and maintain legitimacy and compliance with their decision in a situation where a significant number of partisans are dissatisfied. Discontent is viewed as opportunity for mobilization by the influence group, and a problem to be managed by the system perspective.[48]

> "Authorities become recipients or targets of influence and the agents or initiators of social control. Potential partisans have the opposite role..."[49]

At this point the development or decline of a social movement becomes extremely complex because of separate perspectives, erratic interrelationships, and confusion regarding symbols of communication:

> "Under certain conditions, agents of control can successfully dissipate a movement.....or contribute to movement growth and even attainment of goals."[50]

Social movements face dangers and crisis if their actions stimulate similar action from other groups, and the counter-movement succeeds. The movement may be killed in the minds of the public as a result of negative influence and resistance on the part of authorities. It can also be killed by the authorities through use of force. There is the danger to a movement if the leaders neglect to revise their strategies in the light of shifting circumstances. There is also the chance that the movement will splinter and they lose their solidarity.[51]

There are two apparent methods for authorities to handle discontent. One aims at modification of the content of the decision and the other exerts control over the partisans. Both attempt to remove pressure from the au-

thorities. One yields ground and the other directs coun-
terinfluence.[52] If social control is effective it tends to regulate access of partisans to resources and their ability to
bring resources to bear on decision makers: rewards and
punishment are made contingent on attempts at influence: and the desires of the partisans are changed so that
their attitude toward the political object is altered, which
also increases the power of authorities by allowing them
to regulate their options and increase resources.[53]

Authorities can choose to draw partisans into the
system through participation and cooperation. By drawing partisans into the leadership or policy making structure of the organization the authorities avert threats to
the stability of their existence. It also eliminates control
problems and takes the promoters of discontent out of the
public eye. Both authorities and partisans fear cooptation
because it involves outcome modifications that are difficult to determine in advance.[54]

Cooptation is also a way of maintaining the respect
of those committed to either the system or the ideology
of the movement and avoiding the embarrassment of confrontation, or the possibility of violence. Minimizing the
distance between the authorities and the partisans increases the trust factor, and gives the partisans access to
power and opportunity. Partisans may opt for long range
goals and sacrifice some immediate satisfactions, or they
may risk the loss of followers who have been attracted to
the rebellious nature of the protest movement.

Protest activities, of one form or another, are efforts
to dramatize grievances in a way that will attract attention. Ultimately the expressions of political grievances

will attract the attention of those outside the areas of influence, even in a stable society.[55] In connection with black militancy and collective violence the studies indicate there was more non-violent black protest, "despite the popular impression conveyed by the emphasis of the news media on episodes of spectacular violence or threats of violence."[56]

As a result of militancy or violence and agitation the courts become a central political forum. The courts are organized to perform the task of adjudicating, and civil disturbances require them to "deal with the outcome of political conflict as if it were only a criminal matter. Under such conditions, they often become and are perceived as an instrument of power rather than of law."[57]

Gamson suggests that when "authorities begin identifying with alienated groups and their causes, presumably changes can come without influence 'from below.' Until that day, a little influence helps."[58] In addition, those who pursue the study and reportage of mass movements, and collective behavior might take a look at Marx and Wood's list of twenty-two categorical imperatives, specifically the following:

II.   Thou shalt study social movements in their organizational and environmental contexts.

VI.   Thou shalt bring a compassionate skepticism to publicly available data on any given movement.

XI.   Thou shalt try to relate conditions of social strain to people's perceptions of strain and to their participation – or lack of participation – in collective behavior activities.

XII. Thou shalt not confuse leaders with followers,

XIII. Thou shalt be more sensitive to types of social movement participation and thou shalt not confuse followers with sympathetic bystanders.

XIV. Thou shalt be aware of the possible uses and misuses of research on social movements."[59]

This chapter has focused primarily on the manner in which power and control fluctuate and are distributed. Those who govern and/or possess wealth have access to large amounts of power. Those who wish to change the system, as participants in a mass movement, may hold very little actual power, in terms of authority or resources, but depend on their numbers, their dynamics, and the media coverage of their activities to gain public attention and apply pressure. The next chapter will investigate the latter source of power, media coverage, by defining the media's power to inform and influence, along with determining some areas of media responsibility.

III
MEDIA –
POWER AND
RESPONSIBILITY

At the end of the work day the average American kicks off his shoes and lounges in front of a warmed up television set, with remote control, snacks and drinks within easy reach. A commercial interrupts his favorite program or football game. A chubby brown-robed smiling monk places a stack of manuscript pages in a machine, and views with amazement as the pages are duplicated and collated. Another interruption shows a roomful of college students cheering when told they can now get 1,000 anywhere, anytime minutes on their cell phones.

When the late, late movie or talk show ends the TV watcher clicks the "off button," and while he sleeps the gigantic presses of the city newspaper roll out the early morning news to greet him in print over coffee and toast at the breakfast table. On the way to work our average American listens to the radio play music and lets him know what kind of weather to expect that day; gives him traffic reports and periodic news reports. Arriving at the office, our commuter checks the E-mail on his personal computer and makes a plan for the day's activities.

For the most part the average American accepts passively the information received and the technology of the particular medium carrying the advertising, news and entertainment messages to him and to millions of other average Americans. He is only vaguely aware of the impact and changes occurring in the culture, and the communication process representing a learned and shared behavior.[1]

This chapter will explore some aspects of the oral and linear culture channels of communication, the American tradition of reporting news, and some of the changes that have occurred in journalism over the past decades leading up to the arrival of the American Indian Movement and other mass movements on the scene. The chapter also examines the power of the media in relationship to content and form, and the responsibility of the media representatives and media consumers in seeking truth.

Cultural History

Marshall McLuhan became a vocal critic regarding the effect of the medium as well as the message content, and Harold Innis believed it necessary to study media characteristics to appraise their effect on culture. Innis makes the assumption that:

> "The use of a medium of communication over a long period will to some extent determine the character of knowledge to be communicated....Its pervasive influence will eventually create a civilization in which life and flexibility will become exceedingly difficult to maintain and that the advantages of

a new medium will become such as to lead to the emergence of a new civilization."[2]

The mystery of how people learn to learn continues to be unraveled by psychologists, sociologists, political scientists and communication specialists, and it touches all the other academic disciplines in one way or another. The differences in learning continue to present difficulties that have to be overcome whenever two people who have been raised in different cultures begin to interact for more than the shortest period of time.[3] Some of the difficulty occurs as a result of a tendency on the part of people of the Western world culture orientation to fail to grasp the extent to which religion and religious symbols are integrated into the lives of people from the Eastern world. The degree of integration may vary from one culture to another.[4]

In the United States, as an example, the American Indian has suffered the effects of the perceptions of the white man, who has viewed him out of the context of his own culture. Innis describes the condition of the Indians living miserably depressed lives on reservations as wards of the government:

> "Most of these Indians had neither the dignity of their old ways nor the advantages of the now dominant society that surrounded them. Up to this point it had been government policy to treat all the different tribes alike, as if they were ignorant and somewhat stubborn children..."[5]

The conquering white man failed to see the Indian as an already integrated personality, but rather preferred to teach him the new ways for his (the Indian's) own good. The Indian experienced the condition known as "culture shock" in the land of his birth. Familiar cues were replaced or removed. He was now forced to learn new symbols of communication and new networks for communicating messages.

Culture is many things. Edward Hall, in *The Silent Language*, discusses the close link between man and his culture:

> "Culture **is** communication and communication is culture....Culture is concerned more with messages than it is with networks and control systems.... Man operates on three different levels, the formal, informal and technical....Experience is something man projects on the outside world as he gains it in a culturally determined form....Probably the most difficult point to make and make clearly is that not only is culture imposed upon man but it **is** man in a greatly expanded sense."[6]

There appear to be two divisions of culture and communication: the oral tradition and the linear (or written) communication. Although the oral tradition served the world well for thousands of years the introduction of print placed those still lingering in their traditional channels of communication in the primitive category of the unlearned.

It is interesting to note that although Christianity in the Western cultural tradition leans heavily on the printed word for the transmission of its message, its founder, Jesus Christ, favored the oral tradition. He used the oral-tradition story telling channel of communication and trusted his followers to transmit his messages accurately. Christ left no personally recorded messages, despite the fact that communication symbols and tools were at his disposal and he was reported to have quoted and interpreted Old (Hebrew) Testament scripture among and to the most learned. The only mention of Christ writing anything down was when he supposedly detailed the "sins" of the men waiting to stone the adulteress woman to death, and those words would hardly be considered primitive by modern standards.

It is also interesting to note that the American Indian had developed a sophisticated system of sign language utilized within and between tribes. They had developed picture symbols that not only decorated clothing, body and dwelling, but also conveyed message and meaning. According to sociologist Tamotsu Shibutani those channels of communication consist of more than mere points of contact. The symbols and their use also consist of shared understandings about who may address whom, about what subject, under what circumstances, and with what degree of confidence.[7]

The modern Western language-technology development is as interrelated as the symbol-communication channel systems of the oral cultures. People of the oral culture tradition may experience a feeling of distrust regarding the modern technological approach to memory banks, information storage and record keeping. As far back as the fourth century, Plato tried to preserve the remnants of the Greek culture in the style of the Socratic dialogues, and warned against putting wise thoughts into writing and

rendering them unalterable. Plato's thoughts on the subject were set down in Aristotle's seventh epistle:

> "No intelligent man will ever be so bold as to put
> into language those things which his reason has
> contemplated, especially not into a form that is
> unalterable – which must be the case with what is
> expressed in written symbols."[8]

The development of language and technology gave
man the tools to divide the world and conquer, store knowledge and discover the secrets of nature – but the impact of
writing and printing on modern civilization also increased
the difficulties of understanding civilizations and cultures
based on oral tradition.[9] The development of the calendar,
clock and other means of patterning existence by divid-
ing life into years, months, days, hours, minutes and even
seconds has become so widely accepted that it is difficult
for the time-oriented people to understand space oriented
cultures where people live by seasons, light and dark, and
rebel against what they consider artificial divisions.[10]

Americans in particular, have become task masters at
segmenting and scheduling time and are oriented almost
entirely toward the future, favoring newness and possess-
ing a tendency to be preoccupied with change. This short-
ened perspective limits the consideration of long term
projects, "such as sixty and one-hundred-year conserva-
tion works requiring public support and public funds."[11]

Thousands of years of communication effort brought
mankind from the spoken word, through hieroglyphic
script, into phonetics and the solar year – marking time

and ruling lines, development of an alphabet and numeric system to aid trade and commerce, letters to replace images for the Hebrews, stone tablets, papyrus, parchment, mechanical reproduction, paper, and publishing as a business.

The world is at the fingertips by pushing a button or flipping a page. Journalist Jean-Louis Servan-Schreiber explains how post-World War II technology has expanded the scope and flexibility for information transmission:

> "If inventions that are the base of modern communications date from before 1940, the multiplicity of refinements made since WWII, particularly since 1960, have given them total flexibility. Transistors, satellites, computers, and photocopying devices have put the world at man's fingertips....News is received from anywhere in the world virtually as it happens, regardless of the subject or where the information is stored."[12]

Mass production, massive education programs, mass media communication, massive political movements – all designed to appeal to the masses (undefined large numbers) of people listening, viewing, watching or reading. The average American home has television viewing at least six hours a day, the radio or radios are on two or three hours each day per person, uncalculated hours in front of a computer screen surfing the Internet or doing E-mail, at least one daily newspaper is delivered, along with magazines for men, women and children, and occasionally a book or its condensed version comes into the home.[13]

People are individuals and not masses, although messages are directed to mass audiences. Advertisers predetermine their target market and direct their message accordingly. The same stimulus (or information) received by great numbers of people may produce a similar action or reaction to those stimuli – and people working in the area of mass media will be the first to admit that the potential for massive influence exists.

Growing right along side of technology-education-communication has been the American tradition of emphasis on news reporting, investigation, exposure and controversy, a free press – free of government control and influence.

The American Revolution received assistance from advocacy journalism working outside the influence of the dominating British Colonial Government's control. The Green Dragon Tavern in Boston adjoined the *Boston Gazette* office and the editors, Benjamin Edes and John Gill, often gathered with the promoters of the revolution and helped to keep the political pot boiling both in and out of print.[14] Early American newspapers, far from being objective, were generally quite partisan. George Washington, the first President of the United States, registered his irritation by his remarks about "infamous papers calculated to disturb the peace of the community."[15] And, later, although the press was protected by the First Amendment to the Constitution it often displayed its youthfulness and irresponsibility.

Idealistically the communications media are expected to reflect the voice of the people, public opinion, but in reality there is a long tradition of media reflecting the views of the publishers, owners, or editors, and a stronger case could be made in that regard. Some claim that objectivity began on a national scale with the advent of the Associated Press, pressure from the public, and the Federal Communications Commission.[16]

The tradition of the American press is that of the news gathering watchdog for the public, particularly critical of the government, and often exposing injustices within the peripheral bureaus and agencies of the system. Conflict between the government and the press emerges from time to time. Newspaper reporters, editors and publishers have been confronted with gag orders from the courts, limiting the information flow with the intention of providing the principals involved with a fair trial. Investigative journalists have had to take a better look at the matter of invasion of privacy and determine who are the "public" and who are the "private" figures, and weigh the risks involved in how they gather and report news and feature material.

The press has faced challenges to their assumed immunities in the area of privileged news sources. Court cases have resulted when reporters refused to reveal their sources, and jail terms resulted when they insisted in protecting their sources.

Those who are in responsible media positions where they are forced to make split-second or hair-line decisions as to what the public needs and wants to know must also consider matters of libel, unfair competition, copyright, regulation of print and electronically produced advertising, public relations and lobbying, circulation, audience, the Federal Trade Commission, the Federal Communications Commission, the Department of Justice, postal service, obscenity laws, fair comment, contempt, budgeting and personnel.

For the short time that Spiro Agnew was vice-president of the United States in the Nixon administration he became a vocal critic of news coverage. The country was heavily involved in the Vietnam conflict in the late sixties and Agnew criticized coverage of the anti-war demonstrators and demonstrations, along with criticizing coverage of the Nixon administration and Agnew, himself. Agnew capitalized on the "rising national distaste for radicals and dissent, and the subtle public distrust of that portion of the press that seemed not to be 'on the team' with government against radicalism [and] began to lash out against the press on behalf of what was called 'the silent majority!'"[17]

The news media found themselves on the defensive, and responses varied from self-righteousness to derisiveness. Some media representatives began a critical self-examination, but many feared the attack leveled by Agnew and others would lead to intimidation of the news media. "As the nation moved to deal with the radical elements in society, the news media were in danger of being caught in the middle...."[18]

The Twentieth Century Fund Task Force detailed incidents of media vulnerability to government pressure:

- Government prosecutors, intent on proving that militant groups were seeking to overthrow the government or to assassinate the President, subpoenaed the notes, tapes and files of a number of journalists and publications.

- The Senate Permanent Subcommittee on Investigations subpoenaed the records of a California underground publication to obtain the identity of the pseudonymous author of a number of bitterly anti-police articles.

- Attorney General John N. Mitchell issued guidelines to his prosecutors designed to limit press subpoenas. Two weeks later the editor of an underground newspaper in Madison, Wisconsin, was subpoenaed in connection with the bombing of the chemistry building at the University of Wisconsin.

- President Nixon called news executives from across the country to a news briefing on the Vietnam war and pointedly omitted major newspapers that had opposed his war policies.

- A number of federal and local intelligence agents were discovered posing as newsmen to collect information about militants, and in a series of incidents legitimate newsmen were assaulted or excluded from meetings by militants.

- Justice Department sought to suppress publication of the Pentagon Papers.

- A committee of Congress undertook to investigate the Columbia Broadcasting System's editing of its television documentary, "The Selling of the Pentagon."[19]

Marilyn Catherine McDonald MA

If the Nixon administration had some kind of unde-clared war against the media, then the media were to have their revenge and show of power when the black cloud of Watergate opened up and rained on the White House. The trouble for the administration began before the land-slide victory for the Presidency – in June of 1972 there was a break-in, burglary, and bugging of Democratic National Committee Headquarters at the Watergate Office Build-ing in Washington, D.C. The event was discovered by a security guard, and exposed by a team of news reporters, Bob Woodward and Carl Bernstein, who won the Pulitzer Prize for their *Washington Post* newspaper. Although Nixon fought the scandal for two years he was forced to yield to the pressure of investigations and resigned as the thirty-seventh President of the United States on August 9, 1974 – twenty-one months after his landslide re-election.[20]

Spiro Agnew had been forced to resign as Vice-pres-ident in October of 1973, for evading income taxes and al-legedly accepting bribes. Gerald Ford was appointed, by then President Nixon, to the Vice-presidency and auto-matically assumed the Presidency when Nixon announced his resignation.[21]

The turbulence of the Sixties gave rise and impetus to new styles, methods and outlets for news handling. The term "new journalism" became an umbrella for the non-fiction-fiction treatment of news coverage, alternatives to traditional markets and a modern "muckraking," reviews of journalism, advocacy journalism, counterculture jour-nalism, alternative broadcasting, and precision journal-ism.

Such names as Tom Wolfe, Jimmy Breslin, Gay Talese, and Lillian Ross were linked to the new non-fiction. Alternative publications such as the *San Francisco Bay Guardian*, *The Oregon Times*, *Texas Observer* and the *Intermountain Observer* presented other points of view and dug deep for expose`. Self-examination of the media was aided by publications like the *Chicago Journalism Review* and *(More) – A Journalism Review*. Every cause had its advocate in the newsroom as individual journalists and teams launched out to make national names for themselves and their causes. The counterculture produced underground newspapers, some as lasting as *Rolling Stone*.[22]

The underground newspapers proved to be more than a communications outlet for radical or disenchanted youth:

> "They have evolved into the experimental proving ground for the next generation of journalists, editors and publishers....Even before these young people have taken their place in the establishment, their techniques and their views have begun to appear in the establishment media."[23]

In fact, media have not only been observers and reporters of events and changes, they have also been influenced and changed by the events and circumstances of the times and the people of the times.

One critic of the media, Robert Stein, speaks with the authority and background from copy boy to journalism teacher, editor and former Chairman of the Society of Magazine Editors. He refers to that change as, "the raw material of journalism. Reporters and editors spend their working hours trying to discover and explain what is new in every aspect of human behavior. The irony is that they do this work in organizations that, for the most part, resist change as passionately as any institution since the medieval church."[24]

Media Power

In our mass media communications age, when vehicles for reporting public opinion also carry the potential for molding public opinion, those in position of authority are, for the most part, aware of the weight of their power and responsibility. The power to inform and the responsibility to report the news fairly and honestly is in a delicate balance.

Sociologist Shibutani discusses the matter of crisis frequency and awareness in mass societies. A crisis situation occurs when "men cannot act effectively together and previously accepted norms prove inadequate as guides for conduct." Frustration arises and emergency action is required.[25] Each crisis generates a public, and that public demands news of the crisis situation:

"News has immediate relevance to action that is already underway, it is perishable....information that is timely....News is news only for those who make up an interested public, and much of what is reported in the media of mass communication as 'news' is largely ignored by various segments of their audience."[26]

Major decisions are based on information and understanding of distant events. In a mass society the people are dependent on their news agencies. "Thus, news agency personnel and those who control them are in a position to exercise disproportionate influence over the definition of crisis situations."[27]

Martin Seiden, an economic consultant and policy adviser to the Federal Communications Commission, National Association of Broadcasters and others has stated that the "power of the media" is a cliché, and that that power concept has been accepted as truth. "It consists principally of the ability to reach a phenomenal number of people at the same time." He discounts the influence factor as unproven:

> "The existence since the dawn of history of mass movements and totalitarian regimes indicates that political and social ills would still exist, with or without mass communications....Perhaps we have forgotten that the key to influencing people is, after all, ideas rather than technology.[28]

United States Senator Daniel Inouye, D-Hawaii, holds an opposing view to that of Seiden. Inouye believes media has power. He suggested to a meeting of the members of the National Association of Broadcasters that they also be subjected to the requirements of the disclosure law, and submit routine public statements regarding their income and assets. He said the law should apply to TV anchors as well as politicians because:

"TV has the power to do good or evil, to make or break a politician: the power to elect or defeat the president of the U.S., if you wanted to. You are the most powerful segment in the country....The people who really run the country are the broadcasters. They are the opinion molders. Ninety-six percent of the people in the United States watch television."[29]

Inouye cited the selection of what to cover and report as a means of controlling the news flow. He said that when television network officials appear before his committee on communications the media are there with cameras, but when other sessions are open to the press – "no one shows up. But that is when we were deciding how much foreign aid would be allocated to Israel, Mozambique and others, and what to do about Angola. Maybe you have decided these hearings don't sell advertising."[30]

Critics within the media have been as vocal as the Senator from Hawaii regarding the need for media self-examination. In his book, *Media Power*, Robert Stein quotes a section of Walter Cronkite's address to a gathering of journalists following the verbal attacks by Vice-president Agnew, "....I don't think it is any of our business what the moral, political, social, or economic effect of our reporting is. I say let's get on with the job of reporting the news – and let the chips fall where they may. I suggest we concentrate on doing our job and telling it like it is...."[31]

Journalism teacher-author, Stein, takes exception to Cronkite's view of "it" as in telling it like it is:

"'It' – reality – is what happens to people all over the
world twenty-four hours a day. News comes down
to selecting a small fraction of the day's events.
Those choices themselves have profound moral,
political, social and economic effects. That they
are made unconsciously by 'professional' standards
does not relieve those who make them of some responsibility for the effects."[32]

People in one medium of communication can be
affected or influenced by the information selection and
emphasis broadcast or printed by others. In Servan-
Schreiber's book, *The Power to Inform*, the author points
to the hypothetical newspaper editor-in-chief who goes to
the office already having watched television or heard radio
reports on the top news stories for the day. Adding those
reports to the yards of wire service and agency copy waiting for him he begins to form his ideas regarding the same
information his counterparts at other publications will be
viewing as news.[33]

Media critic Servan-Schreiber cites examples of
spectacular events causing chain reactions. When the first
Vietnamese bonze set himself on fire and burned to death
in protest against American involvement in that country
the picture and story were carried in papers around the
world. Similar events later occurred in France, Czechoslo-
vakia and the United States. Air piracy or sky-jacking also
seem to run in groupings. When one hijacking is headlined several more attempts follow.[34]

People who provide news coverage are forced to make
selections. In 1968 Jacqueline Kennedy Onassis landed in
New York after her marriage and the visit was big news.

Marilyn Catherine McDonald MA

Only the *New York Times* reported on a press conference that same day when a relief worker predicted that two million Biafran children might die in the near future. The media critic, Stein, says that such news choices are made every day and that the people who make them "shape our consciousness. No matter how impartially they report the facts, their choices both reflect and help determine the kind of people we are."[35]

Often the strongest critics of the media have learned to use the media to their own advantage. Politicians running for office need all the exposure they can get and would prefer to address themselves to thousands through the newspaper page or to millions over the television or radio, rather than speak to a half-filled auditorium after hours of travel and hastily downed meals.[36] "The communications media are extremely powerful in city politics. In granting or withholding publicity, in determining what information most people will have on most issues, and what alternatives they will consider in response to issues...."[37]

At this point discussion of the political use of the media extends to the area of protest leadership and mass movements. Studies regarding the relationship between the publicity a protest activity receives outside the immediate area of protest and the duration or effect of, and on, the protest have generated a hypothesis by Gelb and Palley in their book *The Politics of Social Change*:

> "When protest tactics do receive coverage in the communications media, the way in which they are presented will influence all other actors in the system, including the protesters themselves. Confor-

mity to standards of newsworthiness in political style, and knowledge of the prejudices and desires of the individuals who determine media coverage in political skills, represent crucial determinants of leadership effectiveness."[38]

Allen D. Grimshaw's *Racial Violence in the United States* presents a sociological examination of the role of media in relationship to violence:

"The national crisis produced by escalated riots warranted massive coverage according to existing standards of mass media performance. However, the result had a secondary effect of bringing into the scope of coverage violent events which would not have been reported under normal circumstances. Likewise, the media have been criticized for imbalance in coverage and for not adequately reporting successful accomplishments in police and law enforcement agencies."[39]

Grimshaw admits that knowledge of the "riot would spread in any case, but immediate, extensive and detailed coverage both speeds up the process and gives it a special reality." That image of reality tends to reinforce and legitimate participation:

"To generate mass media coverage, especially television coverage becomes an element in the motivation of the rioters. The sheer ability of the rioters to command mass media attention is an ingredient in developing legitimacy...."[40]

Marilyn Catherine McDonald MA

Journalist-media critic, Servan-Schreiber, examines the media's part in amplifying and accelerating the ideas propagated by social order critics:

> "Even in the hands of conservatives or controlled by government, newspapers, radio, and television inevitably play the role of the troublemaker by exposing the absurdities and injustices....This power is, in its very essence, anarchic in that it is beyond the control of any society claiming to be free. It works according to a logic of its own in which exaggeration and one-upmanship combine with integrity and analysis. Trying to check this power on the grounds that it is sometimes faulty or exaggerated amounts to preferring ignorance...."[41]

Functioning within the limitations of a medium of communication carries some built-in impossibility. There are a given number of pages available in a newspaper or magazine. The number of pages is generally dictated by finances, and in most cases advertising revenue determines how many dollars are available as there are few publications surviving on subscription income alone. Radio and television sell time in order to exist, and information or news spots are necessarily brief and often sandwiched between commercials. Even the most objective reporter is forced to make choices among the facts at his disposal for reasons of time and space limitations. The facts are arranged in order of importance, and then the editor decides where the story will appear. It may appear prominently, with an appealing headline or relegated to the oblivion of the back pages. The same is true of radio and television news coverage, the most important stories receive top billing, emphasis in advance treatment and additional time.[42]

Media Responsibility

Journalists have been caught in the middle of two conflicts and power struggles. "The first is the traditional one that opposes them to the government....The second, more surprising and less talked about, is a growing credibility gap."[43] For a time the public lost faith in the media, due in part to the Agnew attacks, Vietnam reporting, and a reflection of the government's position in regard to the media. Meanwhile the reporter tries to meet a responsibility to the public and to his own journalistic integrity by sifting through facts and rumors in determining what makes news and what is true.

Servan-Schreiber has come to the conclusion that there is often little relationship between what "has taken place and what is carried in the media" because of the inevitable errors resulting from the gathering and interpreting of information. He believes that truth is subjected to conditions inherent within journalism:

> "The very conditions of the journalistic profession inevitably destroy news content. News has to be written for deadlines, which can affect niceties of accuracy. Space limitations also restrict the advantages of a full account of any event, with all the shadings that might emerge. Headlines also play a part in coloring the news....At the same time, the story must be simplified, which means that factors tending to modify snap judgments will be left out."[44]

Marilyn Catherine McDonald MA

Reality, or truth, is difficult to capture and report in a mass society where there is a frequent flood of information. One of the hazards is that the time it takes to receive the volume of information leaves little time to "evaluate it and formulate original or new ideas....Mass information, potentially an invaluable aid to knowledge and culture has become a form of forced feeding for whole peoples."[45] The mass society tends to stress the short term or the immediate, and "American sociologists attributed most of the racial and social strife that has swept their country in the 1960s to what they termed 'the revolution of rising expectations.'" So that, while progress was being made in living conditions the people were increasingly aware of what was still to be gained. Television shows, ads and images were presented that left the individual experiencing a gap between what they had and what they wanted or needed.[46]

Shibutani, in discussing the matter of rumor as improvised news, considers all knowledge as tentative and hypothetical:

> "Symbolic representations are not exact replicas of what is 'out there:' they are reconstructions of the real world, which is there and has a recalcitrant character. The ultimate criterion for the acceptance of any definition, regardless of the channel in which it developed, is pragmatic...."[47]

When the news needs of a particular public are not being supplied through institutional or formal means of communication then rumor construction occurs:

"Demand for news is positively associated with intensity of collective excitement, and both depend upon the felt importance of an event to its public.... when balancing of supply-demand is restored rumors disappear."[48]

When people are continually faced with ambiguous situations they become sensitized to news that helps them get their bearings. Because of their dependence on news sources there is an increased tendency for them to be more easily manipulated by propaganda, and unsubstantiated evidence or testimony. The study of rumors takes on importance because of what it reveals about mass movements and social change. Protest, crisis, news, rumor, politics, power, and change are all tied closely together, and there is as much difficulty separating them as there is in putting them all back together for a complete picture of an event as it fits into a process.

In the newsperson's attempt to gather news, ask questions, and get a feel for the people and the situation – in that very effort to be objective, the presence of media people can change the event. Especially in the case of the obvious presence of the television newspersons – the camera tends to change the behavior of people. The media was criticized for "pack journalism" when some 200 newspersons descended upon the city of Louisville in September of 1976 to cover the school busing crisis. Their presence intensified the crisis. William Gerald Smith, assignment editor for WCKY-TV at Louisville, Kentucky, said it bothered him to see the ability of television to spur action:

"We feel we have a responsibility to report the news....All news people are in the business of reporting news, not making."[50]

Robert Stein accuses television of unwittingly introducing values into the news, indirectly:

"While well-groomed announcers were giving us newspaper-like abstractions, the little screen has been showing us death, suffering, and human anger. The connection between power and values, which the journalists, in their best professional manner, avoid making, is nevertheless being made in our nervous systems....and we are beset by media-elected spokesmen to counter the professional politicians, Weathermen, Yippies, hard hats, Black Panthers, police unionists, environmental apocalyptists, Mafia statesmen, Jewish commandos, American Indian occupation forces, Women's Lib guerrillas – all making their power plays on the evening news and the next day's front pages."[51]

Stein says that it is the media's failure to understand their role in the language of power that has brought them under fire from left, middle, and right in society because all resent the picture of the world they're getting.

Martin Seiden, author of *Who Controls the Mass Media?*, bases the power of the media on its credibility, and objects to the impropriety of reporters, editors, publishers, or media owners participating in events they report:

"So great is the activist urge today that many journalists have even gone beyond advocacy and have become actual participants in the event – in effect, have themselves become news makers."[52]

The matter of journalist involvement has been a concern to sociologists as well as media representatives. An examination of the reporter's role requirements by Gelb and Palley has determined that reporters are motivated by:

"The desire to contribute to civic affairs by their 'objective' reporting of significant events.
The premium they place on accuracy.
The credit which they receive for sensationalism and "scoops."[53]

The Gelb and Palley study says that there are difficulties in accommodating these role requirements when they demand newsworthiness, reliability and verifiability of their subjects. In fact:

"Factual accuracy may dampen newsworthiness. Sensationalism, attractive to some newspaper editors, may be inconsistent with reliable, verifiable narration of events....[54]

Reporters on big city newspapers assigned to "beats" sometimes develop close relationships with their news subjects. A mutuality of interest may cause the reporter to make news choices leading away from objectivity. On the other hand the reporter may be at odds with the views of the news subject and this relationship may color the news selections.

Marilyn Catherine McDonald MA

Objectivity in reporting may not only be difficult and in some cases impossible, but it may also be undesirable. Robert Stein says that too much is being asked of media people when they are expected to report reality and also hold the world together:

> "Yet, more and more, as other institutions default and Media Power grows, that seems to be their assignment....How media people use their lives is at the heart of all the questions about freedom and responsibility....under the constant demands of deadlines and competition, their private values tend to be pushed further and further into the background until, in some cases, particularly at the executive level, they disappear completely."[55]

Stein adds that the best protection for editors and reporters from their own qualms and scruples is being hard nosed:

> "Unfortunately....provided by the meanest kind of certitude. Taking too generous a view of human actions and motives exposes a journalist to the risk of appearing naïve. There is no comparable penalty for nastiness – at worst, he earns grudging respect as a hard-nosed reporter or editor."[56]

The sociologist discussing media coverage of crisis situations where violence exists asks the mass media to "develop techniques of reporting which disseminate the essential news, but yet do not serve to weaken patterns of social control or to legitimate resort to violence."[57]

The media critic, Stein, says that what we need most are journalists who:

- Will not limit themselves to any preconceived approach.
- Will use popular clichés as starting points for investigation rather than shorthand to cut off debate.
- Will not be satisfied to accept uncritically the self-serving statements of official spokesmen or to put words into the mouths of bewildered bystanders.
- In approaching complex subjects will use the resources of social science without embracing its pretensions.
- Knowing there is no absolute truth to be discovered in any situation, will nevertheless persist until they have all facts and clues available.
- Will see their work, not as producing plausible little packages of words and images, but as observing and responding to the world as human beings and conveying what they see and feel to other human beings.[58]

The public cannot rest its own responsibility for discernment on the shoulders of media representatives. Placed in the center of "future shock" over-choice, information overload, and advancing technology, the news consumer may panic and opt for ignorance and isolation rather than exert the necessary intelligence for becoming selective and critical in his listening, viewing, and reading.

Marilyn Catherine McDonald MA

The information-consuming public could take a cue from media-aware institutions like the Columbia Graduate School of Journalism where an attempt is being made to:

> "Bring practical experience and academic skills to bear on real problems and possibilities presented by such developments as the New Journalism, the underground press, changing technology and the conflict of government and media."[59]

Professor William L. Rivers of Stanford points out new programs are needed:

> "....not only to train future journalists, but because students generally need to be fortified against the perils of living in a world that is enveloped, if not drowned, in mass communications."[60]

In order for mass media communication of news information to perform an efficient and effective service it will take the cooperation of citizens and journalists:

> "....simultaneous development of a generation of both journalists and educated citizens with increased awareness of the social issues surrounding Media Power and the alternatives available to deal with them. If journalism is to maintain any human scale in a mass society, we will need critical readers, viewers as well as talented editors and reporters."[61]

A journalist's perceptions are individualistic, precious possessions, and the integrity of those perceptions faces the same conflicts and challenges experienced by every other human being in a mass society. Keeping the journalist free from political manipulation and organizational pressures assures a clear, honest look at the world on behalf of the public. It is the responsibility of the professionals, as well as the public, to protect and perpetuate the mass media of communication and increase the potential for human freedom and growth.[62]

IV
AMERICAN INDIAN CULTURE

Long before the white man came to the North American continent the Indian lived off the land, held it sacred, and sought harmony with his fellowman. In the name of Christ, culture, and civilization, many injustices have been committed by the white man against the land and its indigenous peoples.

To achieve any degree of understanding of the situation as it exists today it seems necessary to explore the heart and spirit of the people who have been forced to cope with the impact of their culture being worn away as a new one gradually took over. Now, many suggest, the traditions are returning. Vine Deloria, a prolific and respected Sioux Indian writer, believes that the communications gap existing between peoples and cultures can best be closed through a better understanding of man's relationship to the land he occupies:

"We cannot review the past without understanding that symbols and tactics used to communicate them depend upon a new vision of the nature of man. This can only be possible by creating a new mythology of creation itself. The current fascination with ecology is one key to a new mythology because it attempts to understand the real natural world as a part of us and we a part of it. The key to the communications gap is thus really quite simple. Communications have made the continent a part of the global village. The process must be reversed. The land must now define the role communications can play to make the country fruitful again."[1]

Deloria defines some of the basic cultural differences between the Indian and the white man regarding their concepts of individualism, ownership of property and resources, and social recognition:

"White Americans speak of individualism on an economic basis. Indians speak of individualism on a social basis. While the rest of America is devoted to private property, Indians prefer to hold their lands in tribal estate, sharing the resources in common with each other. Where Americans conform to social norms of behavior and set up strata for social recognition, Indians have a free-flowing concept of social prestige that acts as a leavening device against the building of social pyramids."[2]

The Indian culture has its profoundly spiritual nature that permeates even the modern movements toward social change and seeking recognition for Indian causes. The political polarization of the national Indian movement is understood by Indians to be, at the deepest level, a spiritual and cultural confrontation between Indians and the rest of society.[3]

"America needs a new religion. Nearly every event and movement today shows signs of fulfilling this role, but none has the centered approach that would permit it to dig its roots in and survive. I'm not advocating a return to Christianity. That 'religion' has had two thousand years of bloodshed and hypocrisy, and has failed to do anything more than help turn men into machines. We are probably entering an era in which religious sensitivity is expressed in rigorous adherence to the values of racial and ethnic groups – secularization of religious feelings in political action."[4]

Many Indians are seeking their lost identity and rejecting the stereotype of the Indian that has been projected through the years in Hollywood movies, novels, and radio plays – where the faithful Indian companion named Tonto "never rebelled, never questioned the Lone Ranger's judgment, and never longed to go back to the tribe for the annual Sun Dance. Tonto was a cultureless Indian for Indians and an uncultured Indian for whites."[5]

The images of the Indian war chief and naked savage are being revised by modern day Indians who protest that even the name, Indian, is the result of an historical mythical tradition. Columbus assumed he'd reached India, and by the time the error was discovered the word had spread throughout Europe, and "Indians" they became. Deloria gives every indication that the Indian is sick and tired of being studied by the white man, being proselytized, mythologized, and romanticized. "We need the public at large to drop the myth in which it has clothed us for so long. We need fewer and fewer 'experts' on Indians."[6]

Marilyn Catherine McDonald MA

The term, Indian, is often used in a way that implies there is one nation, tribe, or culture – when, in fact, there are many nations and tribes. Although there are many regions, tribes and life styles, their cultural system of communication is based in signs and symbols relative to their sensual experiences. They are an oral-culture people with an aversion to the frozen, abstract, sterile, or printed word-symbols of the white civilization.

Language

The Indian's language of hand signs enables them to "talk with all men, no matter what tongues they may speak..."[7] It is the language among the various tribes. It is also a method of transmitting tradition, stories, and legends from generation to generation, and accompanies the oral transfer of values in the cultural communication system. The Indian trusts his memory; for he has no "talking leaves" (books) like the white man. As the individual hearer perceives differently, the story unfolds in the process. (Spirit). [8]

In the poetic prosaic book, *Seven Arrows*, by Hyemeyohsts Storm, the author speaks of the difficulties in translating the spoken stories of the Plains Indians into the written form:

> "These stories were meant to be told, not written. In this way the teachers, whether speaking verbally or in sign language, were able to give inflections to particular words to reflect their symbolic content.[9]

The author emphasizes the importance of reading the text, with the capitalized words indicating inflection, in a symbolic rather than literal way. He also speaks of the tradition of the Personal Shield carried by Indians as a means of communicating to others who they were:

> "...these shields....were never intended to give physical protection in battle....they represented the individual medicines and clan Signs of the men who carried them. These Signs told who the man was, what he sought to be, and what his loves, fears and dreams were..."[10]

In Storm's book the man of vision-story teller, Hawk, speaks of the way in which a man's Shield becomes clear to him on the prairie of life, a place of danger and discovery:

> "[The prairie] is also a place of beauty. It is a place of adventure. All kinds of men visit the prairie. Some see only the danger. Some see only ugliness. Some seek victims to satisfy their own pleasures there. Some are timid, some fearless, some frightened, but all people who visit this place share one important thing. They share their aloneness. We face only ourselves on the prairie. We can discover ourselves there, or we can simply run with the animals of the prairie, blindly and at nature's whims. The prairie, my children, is life. This camp circle is a different place. Ultimately, a man's true nature and his shield are clear to him out there on the prairie.[11]

The oral mode of communication encourages spontaneous acts of a group nature, such as singing, dancing and story telling, often marking special days and events. In Ben Sidran's study of oral culture and musical tradition the point is made that, "one effect of the oral mode of perception is that individuality, rather than being stifled by group activity or being equated with specialization, actually flourishes in a group context."[12] An example is the yearly Sun Dance of peace and brotherhood performed by the Plains Indians and spoken of by Indian writers as an experience of unity, and also a time of gaining personal strength.

The circle is a sacred symbol to the Indian. Tepees are round, and placed in a circle. Black Elk, the holy man of the Oglala Sioux Indians, referred to the "nation's hoop" that was broken following the massacre and suppression of Indians at Wounded Knee in 1890. Black Elk told his story to John Neihardt in the early thirties, and spoke of the time he came to live where he was at that time, between Wounded Knee Creek and Grass Creek:

> "Others came too, and we made these little gray houses of logs that you see, and they're square. It is a bad way to live, for there can be no power in a square."[13]

In *Seven Arrows*, Storm speaks of the Medicine Wheel way as the way of touching other human beings, the world around, animals, trees and all living things, a way of learning to sing the Song of the World and becoming a whole person:

> "The Medicine Wheel is the universe. It is change, life, death, birth, and learning. This great circle is

the lodge of our bodies, our minds, and our hearts. It is the cycle of all things that exist. The circle is our way of touching, and of experiencing harmony with every other thing around us. And for those who seek understanding, the circle is their mirror. This circle is the flowering tree."[14]

The Vision Quest is the perceptual experiential search for wholeness. That quest takes the Indian seeker through several phases. Those phases are symbolized in the circle of the Medicine Wheel. The seeker travels clockwise, each state has its symbolic color and animal:

Innocence – south – color green – the mouse
Introspection – west – color black – the bear
Wisdom – north – color white – the buffalo
Illumination – east – color yellow – the eagle[15]

As the individual searches his perceptions change. Each person becomes a mirror to every other person and the heart becomes the teacher, as touching lives produces internal and external harmony. Symbolically, the north represents power. The south is a place of growing. The west is a time for changing. The east is rebirth. The individual receives gifts as he travels through each new perception. Those gifts are the "understandings which you now perceive inside yourself, and which you must give-away to the people so that they may also perceive. Then they will no longer be starving for these ways of learning..."[16]

The stories are mirrors for self-discovery. The teacher in the stories may be symbolized by the old man, old woman, little boy or girl, the contrary, the spirit, or Vihio

Marilyn Catherine McDonald MA

(the knowledgeable fool). The teacher is self. The seven teaching arrows are part of the great mirror where pieces are always being fitted together. Stories contain symbols:

Fire = the spirit of the people, the east
Evening = time of rest, dreams, way of the west
Rainbows = the myth created upon the earth
Lake = mirror of totality
Grandmother's braids = experience
White braids = wisdom
The coyote = the gentle trickster
Dragonfly = things in life that hypnotize and cause fixation
Puppies = philosophy
Burned sweet grass = mother earth sharing experience
Lightening = illumination with introspection
Mouse = perceives only what is close to it
Lodge of gambling = risk in daily life[17]

Indian symbolism is tied closely to nature. What the western culture terms months are referred to in terms of moons by the Indians. Beginning with January, Moon of:

Frost on the tepee
The dark red calves
The snow blind
Grass appearing
When the ponies shed
Making fat (when the sun is highest and growing power is strongest)
Red cherries
When the cherries turn black

When the calves grow hair (when plums are scar-
let)
Changing seasons
Falling leaves [18]

The Plains Indian names mentioned in *Seven Ar-
rows* reflect the same colorful significance tied to nature:
Singing Stone, Fire Dog, Lame Bear, Day Woman, Flying
Cloud, Prairie Rose, Standing Eagle, Grey Owl, Painted
Elk, Morning Song, Stands Alone Wolf, Orphaned Yellow
Buffalo Calf, Red Bobbed Bat, Curious Antelope, Jump-
ing Mouse, Singing Flower, Sun Goes Slow, Little Black
Bird, Little Star Woman, Not Afraid of Knowing, Bull
Looks Back and Coyote Runs in Circles.[19]

When the Indians were brought into the western
culture they were given Christian names, learned to use
the clock and calendar, taught to speak and write the new
language, but it was not quite as simple to teach the Indian a new philosophy of communication – the manner in
which people speak to each other.

Communication within and between tribes, and between Indians and Anglos, is about more than written or
spoken symbolisms. Jimm Good Tracks, an Indian Guidance Counselor, has written a paper outlining the Native
American principle of noninterference. He explains how
this principle creates barriers for social workers who are
attempting to practice a form of intervention, as it is perceived by the Indian, who adheres to a principle of self-
determination.

Good Tracks questions the ability of the Anglo to
grasp this basic concept of noninterference because of a

totally different orientation. "Perhaps it is the Anglo's arrogant righteousness that prevents him from grasping the nature of his conduct."[20] He says that Euro-American societies rely heavily on verbal forms of coercion and management:

> "Anglo children appear to be taught by their elders, peer groups, and mass media to influence, use, and manipulate others to achieve their personal goals.... In the most friendly manner Anglos are always telling each other and everyone else what they should do, buy, see, sell, read, study or accomplish..."[21]

The traditionally trained Indian child, to the contrary, is taught noninterference:

> "Complete noninterference in interaction with all people is the norm, and that he should react with amazement, irritation, mistrust, and anxiety to even the slightest indication of manipulation or coercion."[22]

According to Good Tracks, the Indian will usually withdraw attention from an interfering person. When he whishes to speak to a person he will place himself in that person's line of vision until he is acknowledged. If he is not recognized he will go away. Good Tracks suggests that the Anglo child is actually taught to demand attention, whereas Indian Adults refuse to respond to interfering demands.

The guidance counselor advises social workers to learn "Indian time" in order to adjust their relationships with clients:

"Native temporal concepts have no relation to the movements of a clock. They deal in terms of natural phenomena – morning, days, nights, months (from the native concept of moon), and years (from the native concept of seasons or winters)."[23]

Since it is necessary for a social worker to understand the Indian's concepts of time to aid the communication process, then it would also seem necessary for the scholar or historian to understand and take into account these same concepts to put their particular study into proper perspective. Often the social worker, scholar or historian fails to recognize the fact that the person trained in another culture perceives himself and his culture as valid and correct. He does not have the urgent need for change that the outside culture tries to impose.

Language, values, customs and norms bind a culture together. When an alien culture decides to impose itself on a native culture, a breakdown of that bond takes place, and the old culture is gradually absorbed into the dominant culture. New signs and symbols are learned and individuals gradually become weaned from their past heritage. Vine Deloria puts this transition period into more acid terms:

"White culture destroys other cultures because of its abstractness. As a destroyer of culture it is not a culture but a cancer..."[24]

The Native Indians were gradually driven out of their dwellings and away from hunting grounds as the white man sought more and more land for expansion, industrialization, resources, farm land, gold, and power. A series of legislation was passed to take care of the "Indian problem" that left the Indians without a culture, stripped of their dignity, and wards of the United States government. The white man tried to make white men out of Indians and then laughed at the Indians for their awkwardness in adjusting to the new ways.

During the late 1800s, the Indians were in the process of making the leap into modern times – something that had taken the white man centuries to accomplish. Tribes like the Sioux, which had always lived communally from Nature's bounty, were expected to value individual land tenure and free enterprise, as described by David Humphreys Miller in his book *Ghost Dance*:

> "Never an agricultural people, the Sioux were forced by government policy to undertake dry farming in flinty badlands soil under conditions no white farmer would have tolerated....more shattering was the endless confusion of the white man's religion..."[25]

Indians at that time were wearing the cast-off clothing of the white men, clothing provided largely by the missionaries. Young Indian men, and some of their elders, were cutting their long hair, even though the long braids were traditionally considered a source of spiritual power, representing experience and the power of tradition. Long hair had been so much a source of pride to the Indians that they cut off the braids of their enemies in battle to cause them shame. It was later that they were introduced to the white man's method of scalping as a result of the Proclamation by His Honour's Command, J. Willard, Secretary for King George II, in 1755:

> "For every scalp of a male Indian brought in as evidence of their being killed as aforesaid, forty pounds....For every scalp of such female Indian or male Indian under the age of twelve years that shall be killed as aforesaid, twenty pounds."[26]

The white man also introduced the Indian to alcohol, which continues to be a source of trouble for the tribes and for individuals. The Indian was awed by the white man's power, and alcohol represented a form of power. In *Seven Arrows*, the chief, Four Bears, answers the question of whether his children have gone mad:

> "They are crazy on stinging water. This is the last of it, thank the Power. This is more deadly than all the other white men's things combined. Some have even killed their brothers and sisters while they were crazy with it."[27]

Lame Bear, in his discussions with Four Bears, goes on to express his awe over the gifts of the white people:

> "They are people of war! They despise peace! Yet still the Power given them by the Universe is a far greater Medicine than ours! Their gifts of wealth and power are living proof!"[28]

Marilyn Catherine McDonald MA

Black Elk, the Holy Man of the Oglala Sioux, speaks of a period of time when he was nine years old, after the Wasichus (white man) had made the iron road (railroad) along the Platte and cut the bison herd in two. The bison had been plentiful and the people wandered without trouble in the land. Then he speaks of the death of their chief, Crazy Horse in 1877, as a time of deep loss for the people. Crazy Horse was bayoneted by a soldier when Little Big Man tried to get a knife away from the chief. Black Elk speaks of Crazy Horse:

> "He never wanted anything but to save his people, and he fought the Wasichus only when they came to kill us in our country. He was only thirty years old. They could not kill him in battle. They had to lie to him and kill him that way."[29]

It was after the death of Crazy Horse that the Sioux were told to move from where they were over to the Missouri River and live at the different agencies made for them. Black Elk reports of that time:

> "There was hunger among my people before I went away across the big water, because the Wasichus did not give us all the food they promised in the Black Hills treaty. They made that treaty themselves; our people did not want it and did not make it....The Wasichus had slaughtered all the bison and shut us up in pens. It looked as though we might starve to death. We could not eat lies, and there was nothing we could do."[30]

This was the time before Black Elk went to the Ghost Dance at Wounded Knee in 1890, where he took only his sacred bow. A bow not intended for shooting or killing. But when he saw the slaughter of his people he said he wanted revenge, he wanted to kill:

> "I did not know then how much was ended. When I look back now from this high hill of my old age, I can still see the butchered women and children lying heaped and scattered all along the crooked gulch as plain as when I saw them with eyes still young. And I can see that something else died there in the bloody mud, and was buried in the blizzard. A peoples dream died there. It was a beautiful dream."[31]

The Indian perceived himself as the victim of new cultural ways he neither understood nor wanted. His language was inadequate for communication of frustration and statement of need. The white man was not listening, so the Indian turned more deeply into his own spirit and into a system of spiritual communication, a system of beliefs.

Beliefs

For the Indian, the land and religious ceremony are closely linked. Symbolism and symbolic language are means of communicating beliefs and continuing cultural heritage. The beliefs of the Indian people are less clearly defined in terms of dogma or doctrine than those beliefs contained in the Christian cultures, a difference that has caused considerable misunderstanding between the two. Vine Deloria has said:

"Formulas of faith were anathema to Indian societies. Debate over implications of the existence of God and creation, of subtleties related to deity were unknown. The substantial doctrines developed by Christian theologians to explain, define, and control deity were never contemplated in Indian religious life. Religion was an undefined sphere of influence in tribal society."[32]

To the Indian, the land is sacred. Not only does the land (mother earth) provide the necessary resources for day to day survival, it also contains the spirit of past generations and a sense of strength and history. Indians believe that their tribal land was given to them by the Great Spirit. The belief in trusteeship defied the white man's method of acquiring land by purchase or conquest. Many Indian Chiefs refused to leave their land, or left broken hearted, because they revered the place where tribal ancestors had been buried and where sacred events of their religion had taken place.[33] Navaho Chief Manuelito spoke these words:

"My God and my mother live in the West, and I will not leave them. It is a tradition of my people that we must never cross the three rivers – the Grand, the San Juan, the Colorado. Nor could I leave the Chuska Mountains. I was born there. I shall remain. I have nothing to lose but my life, and **that** they can come and take whenever they please, but I will not move."[34]

Indian tribes were moved from their ancestral homelands and made to live with other Indian tribes on reservations. In many cases the tribes were culturally incompatible and inept at surviving in the new environment. Eskiminzin, the Aravaipo chief, emphasized these relationships when forced to take his band of 150 followers to the White Mountain Reservation:

> "That is not our country....neither are they our people. We are at peace with them (the Coyoteros) but never have mixed with them. Our fathers and their fathers before them have lived in these mountains and have raised corn in this valley. We are taught to make mescal, (roasted leaves of the agave) our principal article of food, and in summer and winter here we have a never-failing supply. At White Mountains there is none, and without it now we get sick."[35]

When the Apache chief, Chochise, gave up the battle for ancestral land, he spoke of peace and registered his sense of defeat:

> "When God made the world he gave one part to the white man and another to the Apache. Why was it? Why did they come together? Now that I am to speak, the sun, the moon, the earth, the air, the waters, the birds and beasts, even the children unborn shall rejoice at my words....The world was not always this way. God made us not as you; we were born like the animals, in the dry grass, not on beds like you."[36]

The Crow chief, Bear Tooth, was less gentle in his comments to the U.S. commissioners when they arrived at Ft. Laramie on November 9, 1887, when he condemned them for their abuse of the land and its bounty:

> "Fathers, fathers, fathers, hear me well. Call back your young men from the mountains of the bighorn sheep. They have run over our country; they have destroyed the growing wood and the green grass; they have set fire to our lands. Fathers, your young men have devastated the country and killed my animals, the elk, the deer, the antelope, my buffalo. They do not kill them to eat them; they leave them to rot where they fall. Fathers, if I went into your country to kill your animals, what would you say? Should I not be wrong, and would you not make war on me?[37]

The diminished buffalo herds meant more than loss of food to the Indians. They believe the buffalo to be the closest animal to man, and sent to them by the Great Spirit for their use. The white buffalo, when visualized during the Sun Dance, is considered a great favor. The Sioux Indians believe that man cannot succeed without power, and that power is disseminated to the greater and lesser beings, including the smallest of animals. Only the pure of body and spirit achieve communication with the Great Spirit and controllers of the universe. That power is communicated to man in dreams and visions.[38]

Native American Indian tribes each hold their own beliefs. Their ceremonies are experiential and tied closely to the spiritual forces that govern life, and labeled by the white man as pagan practices filled with superstitions. Missionaries, whose ceremonies were based in Western European religious tradition of giving intellectual assent to a body of doctrinal beliefs, pressured the government to ban many of the Indian religious ceremonies. Some of the ceremonies gradually returned during periods of renewal. The Pueblo Indians' ceremonial year still revolves around the seasons and they maintain a certain amount of secrecy regarding some aspects of their ceremonies.[39]

As whites came to learn more about the Navajo religion and customs the medicine man gained acceptance. A program for training medicine men has become an important part of public health programs on the reservation, where doctors and medicine men often work together on complex Indian problems.[40]

Northern plains tribes have reinstituted their traditional Sun Dance. Ceremonies surrounding the Sun Dance last several days and take place during the peak of summer. Traditionally, hunting bands gathered and pitched their tepees in a camp circle. The Indian men painted their bodies, fasted, danced facing the sun, and pierced their bodies. It was the piercing that caused the government to prohibit the dance. The dance takes place in the center of the circle of tepees where a Sun Dance lodge has been assembled. The open enclosure of upright posts and rafters connects to a tall forked center pole. The forked pole symbolizes man's infernal conflicts:

> "There is a twinness about man, a twinness of his nature. And there have always existed the two parts of the People. It is always the Other Man who

does not understand, or the Other Man who is the one at fault. This other man is represented by the forked Tree, the center pole of the Sun Dance....But the question is always which reflection is which? Which one am I? Or am I both? It is a great teaching, and that is why it is symbolized in the building of the Sun Dance Lodge."[41]

The Sun Dance is the time of brotherhood and unity. A time when the drum beat becomes the common heartbeat and the voices of the singers become ingrained in the minds and memories of the participants. A time when the people stand together, touching, in renewal, facing the sunrise.

Ghost Dance – 1890 Massacre at Wounded Knee

A lesser known ritualistic dance originated in the late 1800s and became known as the Ghost Dance, because those who practiced it believed it would restore them and their deceased ancestors to their former way of life. It was also known as the Dance of Death because "it inspired Indians to die fighting for their hopeless dream of a better life in a world of spirits."[42]

The Ghost Dance received notoriety preceding the December 29, 1890, confrontation at Wounded Knee when twenty-nine U.S. Army troopers, one officer, and an estimated 145 to 300 Indians died. Two weeks later 3,500 Sioux streamed into the Pine Ridge Agency, defeated by freezing weather and starvation.[43]

Ghost Dance researcher David Humphreys Miller, has quoted Colonel Forsyth as saying, "Now we have avenged Custer's death"[44] when the Wounded Knee Massacre was over. Miller, also made the statement that after their "surrender to General Miles in January 1891, the Sioux never rose again....with no serious thought of reviving the Ghost Dance."[45] Miller's work was published more than ten years prior to the 1973 occupation of Wounded Knee by members of the American Indian Movement (AIM), which was, indeed, preceded by the Ghost Dance. In order to understand the 1973 Wounded Knee occupation it becomes necessary to explore the symbolic and historical significance of the site.

Wounded Knee became a sacred place to the Sioux following the death of their revered warrior chief, Crazy Horse. After the bayoneting of Crazy Horse by the white soldier his body was guarded by his warrior nephew, Black Elk, until Crazy Horse's father, Old Worm, could claim the dead warrior more than a week later.

The historian Dee Brown, in his book *Bury My Heart at Wounded Knee*, tells of the long lines of exiled Indians being driven northeastward by soldiers in the autumn of 1877. Several bands of Indians slipped away and headed northwest in an attempt to escape to Canada and join Sitting Bull. The parents of Crazy Horse also escaped. They were carrying with them "the heart and bones of their son. At a place known only to them they buried Crazy Horse somewhere near Chankpe Opi Wakpala, the creek called Wounded Knee."[46]

Miller's research revealed that Wounded Knee drew historical significance from the burial of Crazy Horse, a consideration when the ghost dancers assembled by the thousands in 1890. He said,

"Somewhere along this frozen stream the heart of Crazy Horse lay in a secret place, and the ghost dancers believed that his disembodied spirit was waiting impatiently for the new earth that would surely come with the first green grass of spring."[47]

When Black Elk, Crazy Horse's nephew who had stood guard over the body, saw the thousands of ghost dancers assembled at Wounded Knee in 1890, he believed it to be the fulfillment of his great vision, the restoration of the hoop of Indian nations. And, although the 1890 ghost dancing ended in massacre the vision and prophesy persisted.

The Ghost Dance was a religious movement toward social change, a dynamic phenomenon, sustained and perpetuated by charismatic leadership. Vine Deloria has said that the Sioux have "a tradition of conflict because they were the only nation to annihilate the U.S. Cavalry three times in succession."[48] The Sioux war bonnet has become a national symbol for Indianness, but the war chief concept depends on a combination of religious and political motivation.

During the time the Ghost Dance came into being among the Sioux, their chiefs were in a weakened power position because of their reservation living. Sitting Bull was quartered with the Hunkpapas, Blackfeet and Yanktonnai Sioux at Dakota's Standing Rock Agency. Two hundred miles to the south the Oglalas looked to Red Cloud for leadership. At the Rosebud Agency Chief Two Strike was opposed by progressives among the Brules. Chief Big Foot maintained camp outside the Cheyenne River reservation where Kicking Bear held a dream of restoring power to the Sioux.[49]

Sitting Bull was considered a practicing healer and a holy man of great power. Kicking Bear, who brought the Ghost Dance to his people, was considered a 'medicine man,' but hadn't reached the stature of Sitting Bull. When Kicking Bear journeyed to Mason Valley to learn of the Ghost Dance he carried with him a smooth stone that had belonged to Crazy Horse.[50] He also carried with him "the dream of Indian supremacy and a revival of glorious warfare with honor....of paramount importance....more vital by far than the bringing back of dead ancestors or the return of the buffalo."[51]

It is important at this point to examine the origin of the Ghost Dance, how it reached the Sioux Indian tribes, the events preceding and following the massacre at Wounded Knee, and the role of the mass media (newspapers) at the time.

In 1870 a shaman (holy man) named Tavibo, of the Northern Paiute tribe of Nevada "prophesied the end of the world and the sure destruction of the hated aggressors....promised that the dead would return from beyond the grave to help living Indians populate a terrestrial paradise."[52] The prophesy gave rise to the dance that swept through many of the tribes in northern California, northern Nevada, and southern Oregon. With the help of the dance the Modoc tribe entered a desperate and abortive outbreak in 1872. The dance flared up and died. Wovoka, Tavibo's son, became the hope of his tribe.[53]

Wovoka went away at an early age to cut timber. He did farm chores for Mason Valley settlers, David and

Mary Wilson, who read aloud from the Bible and spoke of the wonders of Jehovah.[54]

Wovoka learned of the greatest medicine man of all, Jesus, son of God and teacher of good. Later, Wovoka joined other Paiute field hands in working farms in Oregon and Washington. During his travels he met the Shakers,

> "...followers of Skokomish prophet, John Slocum, who advocated complete abstinence from swearing, whoring, drinking, gambling and other evils acquired from the white men....they used the sign of the cross, candles, bells, converts swayed in religious ecstasy to rhythmic tinkling of bells and feverish quaking and trembling.[55]

Wovoka was determined to become like his father and returned to Nevada where the Ghost Dance started up again in 1886. Wovoka taught the people new songs, but the dance dwindled away two years later. On January 2, 1889, there was a complete solar eclipse – the day the sun died. Wovoka nearly died with a fever, but was revived and claimed to have talked with God. Wovoka talked of a time when the earth would die, when the Indians would be safe but the white men should fear being wiped from the face of the earth by a flood of mud and water. There would be earthquakes and then the earth would be alive again.[56]

Hundreds of miles away, Kicking Bear sat alone in his lodge for several days following the eclipse. He mulled over the events of the day the sun "died" and the fate of his people as they remained among the few hold-outs against white encroachment and tribal deterioration.[57] News of Wovoka reached Kicking Bear and the Plains tribes by way of a Bannock from Idaho's Fort Hall who was travel-ing east across the Rockies to visit kinsmen who shared the Wyoming reservation with the Northern Arapahoe camp. Later, he and two other delegates made an unauthorized trip to the Mason Valley to learn of the Ghost Dance and meet the messiah. Kicking Bear was converted to the new way and saw the possibilities of a new world. When he re-turned, he faced questioning by the Pine Ridge agent, but refused to reveal the sacred matters to the representative of the U.S. government. He gave this message to his own people:

> "My brothers, I bring you the promise of a day in which there will be no white man to lay a hand on the bridle of an Indian's horse, when the red men of the prairie will rule the world and not be turned from their hunting grounds by any man. I bring you word from your fathers, the ghosts of those who have gone beyond, they are now marching to join you, led by the great Wanekia who came once to live on earth with the white men, but was cast out and killed by them and nailed to a tree when he tried to save them."[59]

Kicking Bear took word of the Ghost Dance to Sit-ting Bull at the Dakota's Standing Rock Agency. Sitting Bull's people were sharply divided in their allegiance to their chief and to the "squaw man" agent they called "White Hair" – Major James McLaughlin. As ghost danc-ing increased, Sitting Bull became known in the press as the arch-villain of a fanatic Indian conspiracy to recover former Indian territories from the whites. Miller reports that the alarm with which the newspapers viewed the new religion was exaggerated:

> "The extent of the new religion and resulting Indian 'Nationalism' was vastly exaggerated in the public mind. Generally uninformed newspaper editors hungrily latched on to the aging chief of the Hunkpapas as the best available material for reams of copy."[60]

Newspaper reports throughout the country were criticizing agents in the Dakotas for "losing control of their Indians" and James McLaughlin started to believe that Sitting Bull was stirring up tribes all over the country.[61] McLaughlin had enlisted members of Sitting Bull's own band into an agency police force. A telegram from the Cheyenne River Agency advised the Pine Ridge authorities that a band of a thousand Minneconjous and Sansaarcs were heading southeast to join the Pine Ridge and Rosebud agency Indians. When the tribesmen assembled on Cuny Table's grassy plateau, called the Top of the Bad Lands by the Sioux, they made camp and numbered in the thousands. The agents and police became alarmed over the assembly and fever pitch dancing.

A few hours before dawn on December 15, the agency police gathered in Bullhead's cabin on Grand River, where Sioux agency police were "made mad with whisky given them by a white man."[62] They mounted their ponies and charged into Sitting Bull's sleeping camp and the aging chief of the Hunkpapas was shot down by his own tribesmen when he resisted arrest. Had it not been for the sustaining force of the Ghost Dance, the Sioux in their grief over the assassination of Sitting Bull might have risen against the guns of the soldiers. The Ghost Dance followers believed in nonviolence and brotherly love, requiring only singing and dancing until the Messiah brought resurrection and revenge.

Miller labels the subsequent Sioux outbreak-massacre as a "Newspaperman's war:"

> "Perhaps no previous conflict in American history was so well covered by the press. Six correspondents remained at Pine Ridge Agency throughout the entire trouble, filling a maw of sudden reader interest across the country with a welter of anecdotes and observations as well a carefully censored blow-by-blow accounts of the sporadic fighting.... With eager alacrity newspapers everywhere were picking up firsthand, though often distorted, stories relating to the hitherto-unknown Sioux traditions and customs. By and large these accounts were merely highly colored and sensational reports which exaggerated Indian savagery and touted the various military commanders."[64]

Shortly before 9 A.M. on December 29, 1890, the battle began at Wounded Knee Creek camp. Indians were fearful of soldiers camped around them and were made to surrender their guns. A deaf Indian had saved a gun and started shooting. When the soldiers tried to take the gun from him it accidentally went off and caused the others to grab their surrendered guns and shoot. Dee Brown reports an estimated 153 Indians and twenty-five soldiers were killed that day. Other estimates put the figure at 300

Indians, including women and children. Miller reports that only one soldier was actually killed by an Indian, who brandished a stone-headed war club. Two weeks later more than 3,500 Sioux entered the Pine Ridge Agency from their stronghold down the White Clay Creek, and gave up.[65]

In 1913, Buffalo Bill Cody promoted the idea of a filmed re-enactment of the Wounded Knee massacre. The film was rarely displayed to the public and "soon after production several prints were hurriedly confiscated by the War Department and their final disposition remains a well-kept military secret."[66]

Several years after the Wounded Knee tragedy a group of Sioux survivors of the massacre and relatives of those who had died erected a modest granite monument above the common grave on the hilltop near the Wounded Knee Post Office. The inscription read:

> "This monument is erected by surviving relatives and other Oglala and Cheyenne River Sioux Indians in memory of the Chief Big Foot Massacre, Dec. 29, 1890."[67]

At the urging of missionaries, the U.S. government banned the practice of both the Sun Dance and the Ghost Dance. Reservation agent McLaughlin, who was a practicing Catholic, called the Ghost Dance "a more pernicious system of religion [which] could not have been offered to a people who stood on the threshold of civilization."[68] When the Indian rituals were banned the missionaries began to imprint "2000 years of sterile dogmas on the unstructured

Indian psyche.... [And] when the great leaders [chiefs] died Indian religion went underground and became like its white competitor, unrelated to the social and political life of the tribe."[69]

The Indian institutions depended on the power of their chiefs as rulers of nations and tribes. With the suppression of the religious rituals and separation from the land where they drew their strength, the chiefs lost power. When the people were left leaderless the young Indians began to look toward the government, and to the cities where there were jobs, for their source of power. Gradually, the family structure crumbled as the young Indians went away to schools and left the reservations to find work. The Indians were forced to reorganize and deinstitutionalize to survive in their reculturalization process.

Institutions

As the Indian population shifted from the reservations to the cities the American public became increasingly aware of an "Indian problem," which, according to sociologist Fred Eggan, has only two possible solutions: (1) assimilation, either physically or culturally, or both (2) autonomy with equality.[70] Although Indians gained citizenship within their own native land in 1924, they are still often regarded as "second class" and in many areas stand apart from the social and political life of the whites. Their demands are still little understood.

America was considered the "melting pot" of cultures. Immigrant groups sought refuge within its boundaries and embraced a new and better way of life by choice. But the Indian became a stranger in his own land with the challenge of adjusting in order to survive. They were treated as "sovereign nations" in treaty-making up to 1871. Many of the tribes became, in fact, wards of the government and dependent for their subsistence. By the mid-1960s a third of the Indians had moved to the cities seeking a new way of life and a chance to make money. Others began a serious effort to improve living conditions on the reservations with a resurgence of cultural interests and a recapturing of lost pride.[71]

Author's Note: All statistics in this section relate to the period of time leading up to the formation of the American Indian Movement (AIM).

When the Indian Reorganization Act was passed in 1934 the reservation people were able to organize for self-government. Groups officially known as tribes are often remnants of larger historical tribal groups that lived in different places. Although there are fifteen Sioux tribes, the United Sioux comprises South Dakota tribes only, and other Sioux groups are excluded from meetings. The tribe has long been faction-ridden and had never reelected a tribal chairman for a second two-year term (as of late 70s) since its organization in 1934.[72]

At the national level the tribes maintain the National Congress of American Indians (NCAI) and the National Indian Youth Council (NIYC). The NCAI works primarily with legislation. The National Tribal Chairman's Association (NTCA) was organized in the early 1970s and follows the same pattern as the NCAI. One of the oldest continuous Indian-run organizations is the League of Nations for the Pan American Indians (INPAI). It is an alliance of traditional Indians of each tribe. They met in Oklahoma in June of 1968 to form the National Aborigine

Conference and discuss a broad range of subjects from religious prophecies to practical politics. The Sioux held Executive Directorship of the NCAI for fourteen out of twenty five years up to 1968.[73]

When John F. Kennedy became President he appointed a Task Force on Indian Affairs, headed by W.W. Keeler, a chief of the Cherokee Nation and executive vice-president of the Phillips' Petroleum Company. The task force report stressed three objectives: (1) maximum Indian economic self-sufficiency (2) full participation of Indians in American life (3) equal citizenship privileges and responsibilities. The report stated that "...Indians can retain their tribal identities and much of their culture while working toward greater adjustment."[74]

In that same year, 1961, the American Indian Chicago Conference was convened. Some 460 Indians from ninety tribes made recommendations somewhat different than the task force report. They were asking for return of their lands and enlargement of their reservations, and protection of their rights against encroachment of state and federal governments. Their major concern was with their treaty rights.[75]

Not all Indians shared the same objectives. The 1970 census found that there were 488,000 of the total 827,000 Indians living on or near reservations and eligible for the benefits of the Bureau of Indian Affairs (BIA) programs. Indians living off the reservations and in the cities represented a new breed with other objectives. They were experiencing the influences of the military surrounding the anti-Vietnam war demonstrations and the black movement. New groups were forming. The first of these was the United Native Americans (UNA), organized by Lee Brightman, who was attending the University of California at Berkeley in the late sixties. The UNA sought individual membership and crossed tribal lines.[76]

The other urban-oriented group to form was the American Indian Movement (AIM), which crossed tribal lines and proved to be threatening to traditional reservation Indian leadership as well as a source of irritation for the U.S. government, and grist for the mass media mill.[77]

It would be oversimplification to assume that there is **an** "Indian problem" seeking a solution. There are many tribes and individuals seeking an identity, a culture, a means for survival. Vine Deloria believes that the hope of the Indian nations resides in their ability to re-tribalism and nationalize with the use of all that modern education and technology have to offer. He proposes a movement reflecting the spirit of the people and suspicious of over exposure:

> "Crucial to change in Indian affairs is the ability of tribal people to understand the implications of a movement over a long period of time. Any movement which begins to exert a significant influence in America is subjected to publicity. Too much attention from the press can radically change the conceptions and goals simply by making the process appear commonplace."[78]

Deloria's statement was made before the impact of the American Indian Movement (AIM) reached its full strength, and before the Ghost Dance again brought the Indian nations' hoop back to a state of repair, before the media were forced to examine their part in the making or breaking of a movement toward social change. The next chapter will examine a combination of factors that brought the media and the movement into conflict, cooperation, or confusion.

V
AMERICAN INDIAN MOVEMENT (AIM)

Chapter II defined the basis of motivation in a mass movement, its goals, structure, and methods of operation. Chapter III examined the cultural history of communication channels, the news emphasis in America, the power of the media to inform and influence, and the responsibility of media persons in the arena of truth and objectivity. Now, an attempt will be made to further relate the two – mass movement and mass media.

As it has already been indicated, there are several negative results that can occur from the interrelationship, or confrontation, between media and movement, such as:

- The planned use and/or abuse of the media by movement leaders or followers.
- Misdirected or superficial news coverage leading to confusion for the news consumer.

- Overly enthusiastic media coverage resulting in catapulting the movement into its next stage of growth, creating a power play with authorities.

- Loss of credibility among news consumers who perceive the news coverage as being created rather than being reported as it happens.

- Disintegration of a movement resulting from the lack of media coverage.

- The evolution of a movement modality that requires violence or militancy for gaining the attention of mass media controllers and producers.

The American Indian Movement (AIM) represents a process, or series of events, that survived because of a motivating philosophy, numbers of people being significantly involved, and the resources to self-perpetuate. The general public views the phenomenon of a movement in segments, media sound bites, or snatches of events. In keeping with that type of consumer perception of news, this chapter and the three to follow will proceed chronologically from event to event in the life of AIM – and indicate media involvement whenever possible.

The events to be examined will include: (Chapter V) the formation stages for AIM, leadership, objectives, the significance of the Alcatraz Island invasion, the Trail of Broken Treaties leading to the occupation of the Bureau of Indian Affairs building in Washington, D.C., (Chapter VI) the "occupation" of Wounded Knee, South Dakota in 1973, (Chapter VII) the testimony of FBI operative Douglass Durham before the Senate Subcommittee to Investigate the Administration of the Internal Security Laws of the Committee on the Judiciary of the United States Senate, and (Chapter VIII) the Dennis Banks hearings and court involvement as reported in the media.

AIM Formation

The ability of the anti-Vietnam war protestors and the civil-rights workers to generate publicity and eventually gain ground for their demands could hardly go unnoticed by the American Indian community. Their tribal representatives had been issuing requests and demands for recognition for more than a century without achieving the anticipated results. Although some of the Indians participated in the civil-rights movement there was a lack of common goals.

Author Vine Deloria indicated that the time was right for a movement among the Indians to gain recognition and support, but:

> "The media misunderstood that the Indian was trying to preserve culture....media, bored with anti-war protests and civil-rights marches, became fascinated with Indians....rather than understanding the protests as a continuing struggle of Indians, the media characterized them as a new development, thereby missing the entire meaning of the protest issues."[1]

Although there was pressure on Indians to join in the civil-rights marches and demonstrations, they saw little hope in getting government policies changed when they had experienced a series of dishonored treaties and policies. According to Deloria, additional pressure came from newsmen for the Indian community to activate itself:

Marilyn Catherine McDonald MA

> "The perennial question which newsmen posed for Indians regarded the absence of demonstrations and protests by Indians. If there were important issues, newsmen argued, why didn't the Indians make themselves heard? Thus it was that Indians were forced to adopt the vocabulary and techniques of the blacks in order to get their grievances serious consideration by the media."[2]

One of the first efforts by Indians to dramatize their grievances for publication occurred in the Northwest in 1964. Actor Marlon Brando and comedian Dick Gregory went to the Northwest and helped organize a "fish-in" that created a confrontation between the Indians and the Washington state game wardens. The fishermen were arrested and the two public figures were released and treated as outsiders.[3]

When Indian people across the country heard about the fishing-rights issue it caused an increase in similar kinds of protest activities. Tribal governments, with an ingrained non-interference philosophy, voiced their objections to the demonstrations. The government took notice of the activity and began to yield to tribal leaders rather than contend with activists, realizing those activists might well be the future leaders of their tribes.[4]

"Self-determination" became the slogan for the Indian social movement following an assemblage of the National Congress of American Indians (NCAI) in Santa Fe, New Mexico, in 1966. Secretary of the Interior Stewart Udall was in Santa Fe to meet with Bureau of Indian Affairs officials, and the presence of numbers of Indians along with demonstration pressures forced the Interior

Department to consult with them and allow them to attend a planning meeting. It was a first-time victory of its kind for the Indians, giving them a power base for moving ahead.[5]

In the fall of 1966, a group of Indians picketed the Bureau of Indian Affairs (BIA) offices in Minneapolis, Minnesota, demanding to speak to Robert Bennett, Commissioner of Indian Affairs, during his upcoming visit with the tribes. Some of the future founders of AIM were among those Indian protesters.[6]

Urban Indians were benefiting from the War on Poverty funds and the Job Corps during the late sixties. When those funds were cut to release more money for the war in Vietnam, it resulted in a wave of discontent and a release of energies. Urban areas became centers for action, and "Red Power" was the cry. The movement was still in its rhetorical infancy of slogans and speeches until a group of Indians mobilized in St. Paul, Minnesota.[7]

If AIM had a spawning place it was at the Stillwater Prison in Minnesota, where a group of inmates discussed the plight of their people and the disaster of alcoholism in their lives. They decided it was time for personal change, and a time of change for their people. When these men were released from prison they committed themselves to helping the Indians living in the streets. They raised funds from church groups to provide for basic needs and began providing social services.[8]

Alcohol represented a major problem for urban Indians, and the disproportionate number of Indian arrests on the weekends caused the group of former inmates to begin a patrol of the streets and bars in 1968. They watched the actions of the police in the Indian sections and acted as witnesses during arrests. Where there was a question regarding the legality of the arrest, the patrollers would go to court to defend and to demand release. The arrest rate was reduced significantly after thirty-nine weeks of patrolling the Twin Cities. These urban Indians knew both sides of the story, inside the prisons and out, and began to respond to speaking tours and conference requests around the country. As they spoke they also listened, and they began to rebel against what they heard.[9]

AIM Leadership

Leaders' names which were to emerge in the mass media following the Minnesota patrolling events and spread out over the next decade were: Clyde Bellecourt, Dennis Banks, Russell Means, Vern Bellecourt, and Russ Redner. In the beginning none of them claimed to speak for all Indians, nor did they hide their prison records.

Clyde Bellecourt, one of twelve children whose father was a disabled World War II veteran, was arrested at the age of eleven for truancy from school on the White Earth reservation and placed in Minnesota Training School for boys at Red Wing. He was in and out of the St. Cloud Reformatory and the Stillwater prison for burglary and other offenses. He received his high school diploma in prison and went to work for the Northern States Power Company as a boiler engineer following his parole in 1964. In 1968, Northern States Power gave Bellecourt a paid leave of absence to work on the inner-city Indian problems through the American Indian Movement.[10]

Vernon Bellecourt, Clyde's brother, was sentenced to five years in the St. Cloud Reformatory in 1953 for his first offense as a teenager, first degree robbery.[11] Bellecourt discovered the contradictions in his life later when he was "trying to be a realtor in Denver and he remembered the ancient Indian teachings that 'land is the mother of all and no one has the right to own or sell it.' For Bellecourt, AIM was first of all a spiritual movement, a search for cultural and spiritual roots, for an identity."[12]

Dennis Banks was born on the Leech Lake Indian reservation in Minnesota. He was sentenced to prison for three-and-a-half years for forgery and burglary. While in prison he made the decision, with other Indians, to redirect the course of Indian history and his own life.[13]

Russell Means has stated that AIM has never claimed to be representative of all the Indian people – but rather, representative of the facts of Indian life. He was born on the Pine Ridge reservation but grew up in several states after his parents left the reservation to work. He attended five different universities and settled in Cleveland, Ohio, in 1968. He says that he is "an accountant. I've also been a thief, a drunk, a computer operator, a rodeo hand, a junkie, a ballroom dance instructor, a janitor, and a farm laborer."[14]

Russ Redner, a Chilula Indian, was brought up by a white policeman and studied police science. He served in the army from 1964 to 1968 with the 82nd and 101st Airborne Divisions in Santo Domingo, Panama, and Vietnam. The government sent him to Detroit for riot control in 1967. The Detroit riots began the study leading to "Garden Plot," a plan which later assigned the 82nd Airborne Division to Wounded Knee, South Dakota, in 1973. When Redner was out of the service he read about the massacre

Marilyn Catherine McDonald MA

of his own Chilula people by the white men in the redwood forest in 1865, after that his loyalties began to change.[15]

Indians around the country began to read and hear about the activities of other Indians in other areas. In October of 1969, the American Indians United met in San Francisco for a convention. The San Francisco Indian Center burned down on the day following the end of the convention. A group of Indians had been planning to take over Alcatraz Island following its abandonment as a federal prison in February of that year. With their center burned out and no place to meet, it seemed a good time to execute the plan. When nineteen students from San Francisco State and the Berkeley campus of the University of California landed on Alcatraz in early November, they were quickly ushered off the island.[16]

Although the first attempt was quickly aborted, the group of Indian students gained recognition for their existence and publicity that was both favorable and unfavorable, depending on the perception of the news consumer. It caused a "flurry in the local press, which did not serve to alarm the white population but which was a virtual call to action for the Indians of the area."[17]

By November 19, nearly 300 Indians, including representatives of AIM, had assembled in the area and landed on Alcatraz. The next day the incident made headlines around the world. Tribal elders publicly denounced the invasion but privately took some delight in the fact that young Indians were making an impact on the federal government. As a result of the pressure of the Alcatraz invasion the government began a program of land restoration. They returned 60,000 acres to the Warm Springs Tribes of Oregon, gave Mt. Adams back to the Yakimas, and Blue Lake reverted back to the Taos Pueblo Indians.[18]

Richard Oaks, the Mohawk Indian who led the Alcatraz invasion, made further plans for additional invasions in key areas around the country. Alcatraz was followed by two years of activism and sporadic landings on federal property, along with demands for restitution. Traditional Indians on reservations began to identify with and join activists. They joined the American Indian Movement (AIM), United Native Americans (UNA), or Indians of All Tribes (IAT). The surge of symbolic defiance of the federal government was causing alienation with some of the tribal leaders.[19]

In 1972, one of the Indian activists read the 1868 Sioux treaty which offered no specific backup for their land demands but promised that "the United States would protect the tribal form of government." To many Indians this meant the reservation governments which had been created in 1934 as quasi-modern corporations were contrary to Indian tradition.[20]

As a result of the new information the activists went to the reservations and talked to the old men of the tribes and gained a new understanding of the Indian way-of-life. They saw that their "salvation and their people's lay in a return to the old ways, the old religion, and the old political structure."[21]

AIM Objectives

Activists, members of AIM in particular, began a program of spiritual renewal based on Indian culture. AIM leaders went to Leonard Crow Dog, the Lakota Indian medicine man on the South Dakota Rosebud Sioux reservation, and he agreed to be their spiritual leader. It was perceived by them and other Indians as a reinforcement of their religious orientation and charismatic leadership.[22]

The urban Indians had learned the language of protest, and now they were faced with learning a new language specific to their heritage. It became a gesture of reconciliation with the past. An article, "Language as Ideology: The American Indian Case" by Frances Svensson describes the efforts of the urban Indian to learn tribal language:

> "To refer to language as ideology is an exaggeration....Yet its emergence as a primary vehicle for political mobilization represents both a natural and widely recurring phenomenon, in the U.S. and elsewhere....What is politically important in the American Indian case is simply, fundamentally that Indian people have begun to identify their language as the core of their culture, and as a key to their never-ending hope of the struggle for cultural autonomy....Language is a symbolic banner of this new American revolution."[23]

A coalition between the activists Indian leaders and the traditional Indians on the reservations evolved within the context of religious ceremonies. "Ceremonials of the Plains Tribes were filled to overflowing. Many were urban activists who had come to join in the revitalization of Indian culture."[24] AIM leaders Banks, Means and Bellecourt participated in the Sun Dance with Leonard Crow Dog and became respected warriors among their people.[25]

The federal government continued its program of co-opting tribal governments following the Alcatraz invasion. They created the National Tribal Chairmen's Association, which Deloria says is a rubber stamp for government policies and the issuing of public statements against AIM.[26] But, the activists continued to gain national media reputations, and continued to watch government promises disappear when protests were finished. AIM had already set a precedent for violence and over-reacting. A confrontation between tribes and leaders over fishing-rights loss led to drawn (but not fired) guns during their convention at Cass Lake, Minnesota, in the spring of 1972.[27]

AIM demonstrated its power in numbers by convening a thousand Indians at Gordon, Nebraska, following the killing of an elderly Sioux from Pine Ridge reservation. Raymond Yellow Thunder had been beaten by five whites, stripped below the waist, and pushed into a dance hall. A few days later he was found dead from the injuries resulting from the beating. AIM's presence at Gordon motivated the officials to take action against the five whites.[28]

During the summer of 1972, Indian leaders assembled at the Rosebud Sioux reservation for the annual Sun Dance. They discussed the possibility of a march on Washington, D.C., a march that would have the impact of a civil-rights march. The following September, the Alcatraz invasion leader Richard Oaks was shot to death by a guard at a California camp. This further mobilized and motivated the Indians from coast to coast. At the request of Indian leaders around the country the activists met in Denver, Colorado, for the planning session of what was to become the "Trail of Broken Treaties."[29]

Marilyn Catherine McDonald MA

Trail of Broken Treaties

Indians had previously caravanned to Washington, D.C., to protest the circumvention of Louis Bruce's authority as Commissioner of the BIA. Lack of results triggered the second caravan the following year, with caravans originating in Seattle, San Francisco and Los Angeles and arriving in Washington, D.C., during the final week of the Presidential campaign.[30]

Because of the frustration that had been building among traditional Indians on reservations the activist recruiters were able to gain the support of many who broke with the traditional rule of silence to join the protest. Contrary to many of the published reports, more than eighty percent of the coalition of Indians which finally arrived in Washington, D.C., were residents of reservations rather than urban dwellers.[31]

When the caravan reached St. Paul, Minnesota, the leaders drafted a 20-point solutions paper reflecting the feelings of Indians around the nation. It outlined a quasi protectorate status limiting the arbitrary powers of the federal government over tribal rights. It also asked that treaties with Indian tribes be honored with the same degree of legal status afforded foreign treaties, with those rights being superior to the laws of the several states, as originally promised.[32]

The Indians planned meetings with the administration, the BIA, and members of Congress to negotiate the nine demands of the Trail of Broken Treaties Pan American Native Quest for Justice, including the following 20-points for solution of Indian grievances:

1. Restoration of constitutional treaty making authority.
2. Establishment of a Treaty Commission to make new treaties.
3. A Presidential address to the American people and a joint session of Congress.
4. A commission to review treaty commitments and violations.
5. Resubmission of ungratified treaties to the Senate.
6. All Indians to be governed by treaty relations.
7. Mandatory relief against treaty rights violations.
8. Judicial recognition of Indian rights to interpret treaties.
9. Creation of Congressional joint committee on reconstruction of Indian relations.
10. Land reform and restoration of a 110-million acre native land base.
11. Revision of 25 USC 163; Restoration of Rights to Indians Terminated by enrollment and revocation of prohibitions against "Dual benefits."
12. Repeal of State laws enacted under Public Law 280.
13. Resume Federal Protective Jurisdiction for offenses against Indians.
14. Abolition of Bureau of Indian Affairs by 1976; a new structure.
15. Creation of an Office of Federal Indian Relations and Community Reconstruction.
16. Priorities and purpose of the proposed new office stated.

17. Indian commerce and tax immunities.
18. Protection of Indian's religious freedom and cultural heritage.
19. National referendums, local options, and forms of Indian organization.
20. Health, housing, employment, economic development, and education provisions.[33]

When the Indians descended on Washington, D.C., without having made prior arrangements for accommodations, it caused considerable confusion. Indians were quartering in the BIA building waiting for results from the efforts of their leaders to obtain housing. The Department of the Interior finally consented to allow the Indians to occupy their auditorium. When the Indians started leaving the BIA building a few of the guards began pushing some of the younger Indians out the door, and the situation changed immediately. The Indians seized the BIA building on November 1, 1972.[34]

The costs of damages resulting from the takeover, along with the additional police force, were estimated at $2 million dollars. President Nixon received the list of grievances and 20 solution points. The Indians were given a letter recommending no prosecution for their actions in occupying the BIA building, and they were given $66,000 in cash for the purpose of returning them to their homes. But the Indians did not leave empty handed. They removed several pieces of office equipment, entire file cabinets of records, and valuable paintings.[35] The return of those paintings and documents was to become the subject of considerable controversy, involving syndicated columnist Jack Anderson and his assistant, Les Whitten.

The public viewed the occupation and destruction of BIA headquarters as a vendetta by urban hoodlums, without seeing the symbolic significance of reservation Indians acting out their defiance of the 1920 Snyder Act.[36] When Russell Means was leaving the BIA building after the destruction, he said to the waiting representatives of the media, "I know you guys are going to have a field day on this," and Eddie Benton, director of the St. Paul Chapter of AIM expressed his optimism, "for once we've got the attention of not only the country, but the world."[37]

AIM leaders hastily made claims that they had valuable information from the documents they removed from the BIA offices. Columnist Jack Anderson devotes a chapter of this book, *The Anderson Papers*, to the story of how the documents were returned, and how Whitten became involved with the FBI. Hank Adams, Asseniboin Sioux, negotiated for the return of the stolen property with the aid of Whitten. Anderson had agreed that Whitten would act as liaison. The primary news value was in the actual return of the documents and not in the information contained in those documents.[38]

Hank Adams held a news conference in which he urged the Indians to cooperate in returning the stolen property. He had no idea the FBI would later regard him as a thief rather than a restorer of stolen goods, although it was a matter of record that Adams was working toward a return of all the property. On, or about, December 1, 1972, Adams sent a large envelope to the FBI which contained identifying information on the paintings that had been returned to the government. There was a credible witness to the sending of the envelope.[39]

Adams held another press conference on December 9, 1972, and on December 11. Jack Anderson's column published a message the Indian leaders had given him for President Nixon. On January 12, 1973, the *New York Times* ran a four-column headline that "An Indian Leader Pledges Return of U.S. Property." John Arellano, a self-styled Pueblo-Apache Italian, placed his Volkswagen camper at the disposal of Adams. Arellano was acting as an undercover informer for the Washington police and the FBI. On January 29 and 30, Arellano and Anita Collins, a Paiute-Shoshone news editor of the *American Indian Movement*, was sent by Adams to pick up a document shipment at the bus depot.[40]

In expectation of receiving the documents, Adams made an appointment with Dennis Creedon, counselor for the House Appropriations Subcommittee on Indian Affairs, for January 31, at Creedon's office on the third floor of the BIA building. Les Whitten received a phone call in Silver Springs, Maryland, regarding the return of the documents. He went to Adams' apartment to help move the boxes of documents and gather information on the return of the properties. The boxes were to go to Dennis Hyten of the FBI, and Adams wrote Hyten's name on the boxes. The FBI arrested Adams, Whitten and Collins at the curb as they were loading the boxes into the car to be taken to the BIA building. The *New York Times* ran the story "US Arrests Aide to Jack Anderson."[41]

The Adams arrest put an end to the Indian cooperation. Anderson saw the arrest of his aide as an attack on the investigative reporting of the team and said "....Haldeman in the White House saw this as another opportunity to intimidate the press..." and that a victory had been won the moment the headlines hit the street. Anderson's telephone logs were reviewed by the FBI, and as a result, Anderson said that a number of his news sources had been intimidated.[42]

In February of 1973, the Senate considered the confirmation of the appointment of Patrick Gray as director of the FBI. Anderson wrote a column opposing Gray, and the appointment was not confirmed. Anderson said that this represented a "victory for the press freedom."[43]

During the time Adams and Whitten were busy with the return of documents taken from the BIA at the end of the Trail of Broken Treaties, a task force was assigned the duty of reviewing the demands and solutions presented to the government. Subsequently, the 20 solution points were rejected by the federal government. This caused a feeling of betrayal. Many of the Indians were determined to go on protesting. Late in February a series of events on the Pine Ridge Sioux reservation led to the Wounded Knee occupation that was to last seventy-two days, take the public's interest away from the developing Watergate scandal, and provide the Indian movement with an extra ordinary amount of media attention.

VI
WOUNDED KNEE
– 1973

There is no apparent evidence that the major confrontation between members and sympathizers of AIM and representatives of the federal government was extensively pre-planned for the Wounded Knee site. But, with all its historical and religious significance it proved to be a dramatic and symbolic site for the evolution from the events that had preceded the February 27 "occupation" in 1973.

Following the "20-points" scuttling by Washington officials, a group of angry Indians summoned AIM to help them obtain justice in Custer, South Dakota. A white man had been charged with manslaughter rather than murder in the death of an Oglala Sioux, Bad Heart Bull, killed in Buffalo Gap.

Custer Courthouse, South Dakota

White magistrates agreed to meet with AIM representatives in the Custer Courthouse on February 6, 1973. When the Indians arrived they were met by a contingent of state troopers. When the victim's mother, Sarah Bad Heart Bull, arrived late she was denied entry to the courthouse. In her attempt to climb the stairs an officer "pushed her in the face and she fell down. Indian spectators responded to the insult and in the melee that followed the courthouse caught fire."[1] Arrests were made, tempers cooled, and the Indians were assured of justice.

Dennis Banks, AIM Field Director, and Russell Means, Pine Ridge reservation resident, decided to go to Pine Ridge for rest and a victory dance.[2] Banks had been charged with "riot where arson is committed" in connection with the Custer episode and later faced an all white jury which found him guilty.[3]

Means had returned to the reservation in 1972 after living most of his life in cities of the west and Midwest. He studied traditional religion with tribal medicine men and began a food purchasing co-op for the people at Porcupine, seventeen miles north of Wounded Knee.[4] Means had gained a considerable following and represented a political threat to the tribal leaders, specifically to Richard Wilson, tribal chairman.[5]

Writer William T. Hanlon offered this description of the reservation where the Wounded Knee confrontation was to occur:

> "Live on the reservation of which Wounded Knee is a part and you soon realize what a fertile ground it is for the growth of frustration, resentment and anger. The debilitating signs of poverty are everywhere. Outside the summertime circuit of powwows, there are few opportunities for social activity. Across the thousands of square miles of the reservation, ordinary amenities such as public transportation or telephone service either do not exist or are hardly satisfactory. The health care and law enforcement facilities of the reservation

would occasion disbelief in most white communities. Academic incentives are few, and reservation schools are generally not adequately staffed to deal with the problems they must face. Housing, though somewhat improved over the past decade, is often substandard. Off the main roads that tourists travel, there are still one-room shacks without electricity or water that serve as homes for usually large families. There are nowhere near enough jobs on or near the reservation to support the ever-growing population. Some families have to depend on government commodities for their daily bread.[6]

Against this backdrop of reservation life Wilson, president of the Oglala Sioux Tribal Council, considered AIM a threat rather than the messianic deliverer, and warned them not to enter Pine Ridge for their victory dance.[7]

Oglala Sioux Tribal Council Chairman Richard Wilson

AIM and Wilson had already engaged in disagreement over the Raymond Yellow Thunder incident in Nebraska. At that time AIM leaders openly criticized Wilson for his lack of support and inactivity, and accused him of being a pawn of the white dominated BIA. Later, when the Custer Courthouse incident took place, Wilson offered the local white authorities the assistance of the tribal police to maintain order. AIM supporters were outraged at the pitting of Indian against Indian.[8]

By mid-February, Wilson had developed a strong police force prepared to protect Pine Ridge against AIM leaders and supporters. Wilson had won his election after a heated and bitter campaign, and much of that bitterness still existed on the reservation. Wounded Knee was the home of the once-proud Oglala Sioux, driven from their ancestral home in the Black Hills and consigned to the Badlands of South Dakota – and poverty. The tribe had long been faction-ridden and never re-elected a tribal chairman to a second two-year term since the Wheeler-Howard Act of 1934 affected the tribal organization.[9]

According to a report in the *Oregon Times* the occupation of Wounded Knee by 300 AIM members and supporters was the result of an effort by the Sioux Indians "to clean up their reservation and make it a decent place to live":

> "The immediate enemy was Dicky Wilson, the 'Apple Indian' and his 'goon squad' of Indian toughs who terrorized the place. The scandalous 'occupation' of Wounded Knee was merely an occupation by the Sioux of their own property. AIM members were there because their help had been requested by the local reformers. The reformers needed help because the government had sent a 'Special Operations Group' to protect Wilson against the impeachment drive against him.[10]

The major issue at Wounded Knee was a rebellion against the methods employed by the whites in the acquisition of Sioux land, in violation of the 1868 Fort Laramie Treaty which required three-fourths adult male tribal member approval.[11] The major issue became absorbed into several minor issues and at times lost in the whole medium of expression to follow. Their purpose for being there was lost in the verbal attacks and counter attacks, the apparent theatrics, attention getting techniques, and sensationalism surrounding the seventy-two days of conflict.

The scene was set for a Hollywood type production of good guys (U.S. Marshals) against the bad guys (Indians). The mass burial grave from the 1890 Wounded Knee massacre was protected and hidden from view behind the white steeple church on top of the hill, acting as a backdrop for rifle-waving Indians who fortified their position with trenches and battlements.

Media Involvement at Wounded Knee

Media representation was to play a major part in the seventy-two day production of events. Television reporters, especially, would bear the brunt of attacks that their thirst for news information had turned them into newsmakers and participants rather than journalists. Reporters credited AIM leaders with a high degree of media awareness and ability to set up news coverage. On the other hand, reporters complained that the government wrote the rules for using the media and they reported their difficulties in gaining access to the Indians' side of the story.

Ted Elbert, reported for the *Christian Century* that the government had restricted coverage:

> "Shortly after the Tuesday night, February 27, take-over, the government sent federal Marshals and Bureau of Indian Affairs police from other reservations to set up blockades on all major roads into Wounded Knee. They forbade access to everyone, including members of the news media showing identification passes, on the grounds that the safety of persons entering could not be assured –

though members of the press said they would take their chances. Naturally, with no reporters able to get the Indian's side of the story the government could issue its version unchallenged."[12]

Elbert reported that on the night of February 28, television crews from three major networks and several newspaper reporters drove to a remote place, parked their cars, and "cautiously walked and crept over darkened hills, through wooded areas and gullies, under barbed-wire fences and over a creek, five miles to Wounded Knee."[13] They were guided on the two-and-a-half hour journey by an Indian who published an antiestablishment newspaper on the reservation, and his son. Elbert said that the Indians were grateful to see media representatives and later expressed the belief that the government would have moved against them with force had it not been for the presence of the media.[14]

Meanwhile, Wilson continued to gain support of fellow tribal chairmen. Webster Two Hawk, chairman of the neighboring Rosebud reservation and head of NTCA, said that there was no way they could allow the takeover and that they had to stand for self-determination. And William Youpee, the executive director of NTCA, wrote Senator Henry M. Jackson (D-Washington), Chairman of the Senate Interior Committee:

"We are dismayed that responsible offices react to militant groups, whose leadership is made up of self-seeking, self-styled, self-appointed Indians who have no license to speak for reservation Indians, and listen to their unreasonable and irresponsible demands and appear to put much credence in them."[15]

Secretary of the Interior Morton issued a statement on behalf of the Nixon administration, stating its support of Wilson:

> The occupation of Alcatraz, Nike sites, the federal office building in Washington, the village at Wounded Knee and others all fall into it. Their effort is symbolic rather than substantive. They believe that the pursuit of their cause transcends their criminal methods. Their demands are vague and change from day to day. They do not represent a constituted group with whom the government can contract or can serve."[16]

Although reporters may have had difficulty gaining access to the Indians' side of the news, media analyst Desmond Smith presents another view in an article in *The Nation*. He labels the Wounded Knee episode a "Media coup d'état" that was staged from the beginning to end, and he compares it with the Black September attack on the Israeli compound during the Munich Olympics – gaining immediate public attention.[17]

Smith reports that AIM militants moved across the huge Oglala Sioux Pine Ridge reservation and took the sleeping town by surprise, and were not welcomed as heroes in the streets. The majority of the residents fled the village in terror and the remaining handful was taken hostage. When AIM moved into Wounded Knee, KUTV, the local affiliate of NBC, was filming the wrecking of the trading post by armed activists. And by the following morning all major television, magazines and newspapers were represented on the scene. In a week's time the foreign press was on hand for coverage.[18]

Smith explains that the whole purpose of a "media coup d'état" is coverage by radio, TV and the press:

> "The coup leaders use these channels to make their demands on the government. A second distinguishing feature of the media coup is that it does not seek to overthrow the government but rather to seize power within the system. It is an adventurist rather than a revolutionary tactic."[19]

Smith admits that this process creates a grave situation for news-gathers "who do not themselves stage events, but become increasingly aware that they are reporting on staged events."[20]

If AIM militants' takeover of Wounded Knee represented a media coup d'état then the government fed into the newsworthiness by its prompt action, or over-reaction, in providing a contingency of marshals, FBI agents and others to number 300. The incident was then catapulted into the evening TV news slots for viewing by 200 million Americans.[21]

A *Time Magazine* article of March 19, 1973, labeled the protest-confrontation a suspenseful show of Red Power... [with] all the elements of bad theater:

> "The Indians insisted on outmoded makeup (war paint) and melodramatic lines ('Massacre us or meet our human needs'). The Federal Government

brought in outrageous props, including war planes. There were too many theatrical asides aimed at the TV cameras and too many studied parallels to the Vietnam War."[22]

The government's show of military force may not have been as spontaneous as media observers might have thought at the time. Three years after the Wounded Knee "occupation" the *Oregon Times* refers to the "Special Operations Group" (SOG) as a secret Pentagon plan code-named "Garden Plot." "Garden Plot" also was reported in November of 1975, on the pages of Arizona's *New Times* an alternative weekly, by Ron Ridenhour, the reporter who uncovered the My Lai incident in Vietnam. The *Oregon Times* article claims that the conventional press ignored the information on "Garden Plot" at the time and ever since.[23]

According to *Oregon Times*, "Garden Plot" had been rehearsed:

> "Military exercises under the code name 'Cable Splicer,' were carried out in Oregon as well as other states, bringing together the U.S. Army, the National Guard, and local police agencies. 'Cable Splicer' was an effort to train local law enforcers in the techniques of counter-insurgency which the Army had refined in Vietnam, and to lay the groundwork for a coordinated military/police response to revolution at home."[24]

Marilyn Catherine McDonald MA

In February 1973, Col. Volney Warner, Chief of Staff of the 82nd Airborne Division, received orders to go to Wounded Knee and prepare an attack plan:

> "Under 'Garden Plot,' the Pine Ridge reservation falls within the pale of the 82nd Airborne....the FBI wanted 2,000 troops to do the job, but Warner, and expert on psychological warfare, had a better idea: beef up the FBI and the U.S. Marshal's forces, including SOB, supply them with military equipment and advice, and let them do the job, preserving the appearance of a 'police' rather than 'military' action."[25]

The *Oregon Times* article further reported:

> "The Defense Department provided the Justice Department with high-powered rifles, ammunition, gas grenades, grenade launchers, high explosives, air delivery canisters, helicopters, jeeps, trucks, armor, technicians and military advisors. Outfitted as a clandestine army, the Justice Department expended 150,000 rounds of ammunition on the besieged Indians in addition to ammo it procured from its own stores.[26]

Spread out over two-and-a-half months of conflict at Wounded Knee would be a series of gunfire exchanges, attempted escapes by Indians, attempted entries by Indian supporters, demands, counter offers, negotiations, settlements, cease fire agreements, and a mixture of public apathy, anger, indignation, and support for one side or the other. Indians on the reservation would continue to be concerned about the security of their jobs and their day-to-day living as they had been before the incident began at Wounded Knee. A news story in a South Dakota paper would reflect the concerns of the area residents regarding the Wounded Knee effects on the tourist industry during the coming summer months.[27]

Rapid City Journal executive director James Kuehn expressed his reporting concerns to writer Terri Schultz:

> "We haven't yet run an editorial about Wounded Knee because we still aren't sure what to think. We've sent our own reporters out there a couple of times, but mainly we use wire copy. We're so close to the situation and things are so tense, you can't say anything about the Indians without offending somebody."[28]

The Schultz report on Wounded Knee was an unraveling of what happened behind the scenes and an exposure of the news coverage – a finding of how most of the press was fooled:

> "All it lacked was truth, a minor failing of major news coverage. In truth, Wounded Knee II was largely a pseudo-event to which the world press responded with all the cautiousness of sharks scenting blood."[29]

Schultz interviewed reservation Indians, as well as U.S. Marshals, and other reporters. On a day when Russell Means was performing for the reporters – having helped direct television coverage himself – Schultz singled out a young Indian man:

> "....with words to explain Indian hatreds and hopes, but no one listens to him. He is a Mohawk, and Mohawks do not speak for the Sioux, even when the Sioux seem unable to speak for themselves.[30]

> "The young Indian described the Indians as givers and the Americans as takers: 'When givers meet takers the givers lose.' His Mohawk name in Kanatekeniate, but he uses the American name Tom Cook. Around his neck he wears a Sony tape recorder for his job with the Mohawk newspaper, *Akwesasne Notes*. So the press interviews the press."[31]

Refugees, hostages, evacuation deadlines, demilitarized zones, armored personnel carriers rumbling over the landscape, road blocks and command posts, and an occasional Air Force Phantom streaking low overhead on a reconnaissance mission. *Time Magazine* correspondent Ken Huff recounted the night before the Government deadline for evacuation:

> "Seven Indian leaders stripped, some naked, others to their shorts, and entered an Indian sweat lodge – a wooden framework covered by an orange carpet and a purple blanket – to receive clarity of mind and body. The warriors, perhaps 150 of them, seemed perfectly willing to die. With the sun setting behind their backs and the chill wind whipping up puffs of dust, they formed a semicircle and watched as the tribal fathers emerged from the steaming lodge.

Alert the Media

"A Sioux spiritual leader named Leonard Crow Dog struck up a chant in the Lakota language. As each warrior passed by, he blessed him and painted a slash or a circle of red powder under the left eye. Each warrior then stepped into a white tepee making a holy sign over the bleached skull of a buffalo head."[32]

Though the Indians prepared to die, it was not necessary, as Dennis Banks shattered the solemnity an hour before the deadline when he leaped out of a blue Coupe de Ville Cadillac that roared up to the scene and announced that both sides had agreed to a cease fire proposed by the National Council of Churches of Christ.[33]

The National Council of Churches later provided observers with white armbands and the NCC logo to take up positions around Wounded Knee to prevent breaking of the cease fire agreement. Meanwhile, the attorneys for AIM shuttled back and forth between the Bureau of Indian Affairs office in Pine Ridge and the AIM fortress at Wounded Knee. After a week of negotiating the Justice Department backed down on its "threat to arrest any Indian militants leaving the trading post and confiscate their weapons as evidence" by removing all 300 U.S. marshals, FBI agents and local policemen.[34]

Russell Means said that he wanted to see headlines that said "U.S. surrenders to Indians" and told reporters that the Justice Department had done the only sensible thing and wondered why they hadn't been ordered to withdraw earlier to de-escalate the situation.[35] On Sunday, March 11, Means announced on national television that the Oglala Sioux Nation had been formed and declared its independence from the United States.[36]

Several days later Marlon Brando gave the Indian cause additional publicity refusing to accept the best actor award from the Academy of Motion Picture Arts and Sciences. A written statement was read (in part) by Shaskeen Littlefeather, at the Academy Awards ceremonies. Brando refused the award for his performance in *The Godfather* in protest against the movie industry's treatment of the American Indian. Brando was later to announce a proposed new film based on the happenings at Wounded Knee. Brando was to have played an attorney in the film and the proceeds from the film were to have gone to Indian self-help projects.[37]

Broadcast executive Desmond Smith expressed the belief that AIM leaders had succeeded beyond their wildest dreams by mid-March because:

1. They totally controlled the village of Wounded Knee, keeping the federal government out, but (by means of back trails) selectively allowing the press in.

2. AIM's activities in Wounded Knee made good copy and even better pictures. The press is always hungry for pictures, and AIM greatly increased its coverage with quasi-military preparations: cleaning weapons, digging trenches, preparing roadblocks, holding powwows, etc.

3. AIM succeeded in broadcasting the impression that – unless the government surrendered to into demands – a second massacre at Wounded Knee was possible. They would kill whites and be killed because (as the Sioux once cried at Little Bighorn), 'It's a good day to die.'[38]

The Indians made no secret of the fact that they were using every ploy available to them to gain the attention of the public through the media. According to Vine Deloria, the attention was long overdue and much needed, as Indians had tried for more than a century to discover how to survive in the white man's system without cooptation, or being consumed by the federal government:

"It seems, however – again looking at events in retrospect – that there really never was a federal policy for dealing with Indian problems. Indian problems and policies were in fact the province of numerous and nameless bureaucrats, none of whom had any desire to do more than keep the natives quiet, or at least to keep them off the front pages."[39]

In the beginning of the confrontation at Wounded Knee, Russell Means outlined vast demands of a general nature:

"The return by the U.S. government of territories in both Dakotas, Montana and Nebraska; the investigation of long-broken treaties and a full-scale probe by Congress of the Bureau of Indian Affairs. But then, Means shifted the main focus to his demand for the ouster of Sioux Tribal Council President Dick Wilson. That issue proved to be more slippery than the larger questions over which the battle was first joined."[40]

By asking the Department of the Interior to interfere in an intertribal matter, Means was asking the government to reverse an Indian move toward self-determination.

While AIM leaders were accomplishing their immediate goal of gaining public attention through media the media examined their catalytic role. Media representatives began to agree, at least in part, with statements like that of Assistant Deputy Attorney General Charles Abelard: "The press has created a climate of undue sympathy for AIM," and a comment by Interior Department Aide Charles Soller: "It could have been settled in a week if it weren't for this horde (of reporters).[41]

A *Time Magazine* article dated March 26, 1973, and titled "Trap at Wounded Knee" quoted media representatives who expressed criticism for their own involvement:

- 'The story has been managed all along.' NBC correspondent Fred Briggs.
- 'We've definitely prolonged the thing.' A wire service photographer.
- 'I first started feeling the Indians were staging things on March 7, while they were waiting for negotiations to continue, young Indians gathered in the tribal council house and lit a bonfire. It was 60 degrees outside.' ABC Producer Bill Brown.
- 'If you think it's staged, identify it or don't use it.' Av Westin, executive producer of ABC Evening News told his people.
- 'There's always the fear of being manipulated....Indians shooting at marshals. [news value]

we have to cover that possibility.' Dick Fischer,
NBC News Producer.[42]

National Review editorials were highly critical of the
Indians, reporters, and the government's handling of the
situation. In a March 30, 1973, editorial Wounded Knee
was referred to as a "fiasco:"

> "The Indians scenario at Wounded Knee might
> have been drafted by Mark Rudd a Sixties happen-
> ing in Wild West décor, bad guerrilla theater remi-
> niscent of Morningside Heights or Spraul Plaza....
> William Kunstler [AIM attorney] and Ralph Ab-
> ernathy [Southern Christian Leadership Confer-
> ence], rushing in from the wings like vampires to a
> blood bank, Tom Wicker [*New York Times*] wring-
> ing his columnar hands, TV coverage 'in depth,'
> clenched fists, even war paint, and savage ceremo-
> nies dredged up for the occasion."[43]

National Review further lampooned the press for their
involvement with a plea to "Clean up Wounded Knee:"

> "TV cameramen have repeatedly rearranged the
> insurgents in more appealing tableaux. Indians
> cooperated by reenacting interrogations, lighting
> signal fires, and staging religious rites to oblige
> the cameramen...AIM leaders early on announced
> their secession for the U.S., a step suggested to
> them by a reporter. Indeed, the certainty of high
> media excitement was obviously one element in the
> calculation of AIM leadership, in their bid to top-

ple the incumbent Sioux leader, Richard Wilson, a pre-McLuhan type."[44]

On May 11, the *National Review* editorialized the breaking of the cease fire when three small planes flew over Wounded Knee and dropped supplies to the militants, claiming that militants later opened fire on an FBI helicopter and federal ground forces. The editorial opened its fire on the press:

"A few deep thinkers were heard to suggest the possibility of some connection between the air lift and subsequent bursts of shooting. Tush, no, said a *Boston Globe* reporter who went along on the flight, only food and medicine, no arms or ammunition were dropped. The reporter's indictment for abetting rioters added a sideshow (Freedom of the Press) to the main event. Attendance is down at both."[45]

The same editorial quoted a woman's question, "If AIM is working for Indian people, why the hell are they burning down our property?" The editorial answers the woman's question with, "Because, of course, they hope to provoke some newsworthy retaliation."[46]

Writer Terri Schultz summed up the frustrations of trying to report an event (Wounded Knee) that occurs in the midst of a continuing process:

"The reporters shredded the stories into pieces, tossed them into the air and recreated them as they fell into designs of their own choosing. We tightened up the facts, smoothed the edges, covered up the blemishes like portrait artists with fussy clients. We wrote good cowboy-and-Indian stories because we thought it was what the public wanted, and they were harmless, even if they were not all true. For, the truth is buried in too many centuries of lies like fossils embedded in layers of shale. Let the Recording of the Event make do as the event – and don't believe everything in the media."[47]

Results

The occupation at Wounded Knee ended on May 8, 1973, when the White House agreed to send representatives to the reservation to discuss grievances with Indian leaders. The government law enforcement had cost an estimated $5 million dollars. Sporadic gunfire over the seventy-two days resulted in the death of two Indians and injuries to a U.S. marshal, a Federal Bureau of Investigation agent, and a dozen Indians.[48]

When residents of Wounded Knee returned they found "an estimated $240,000 of damage done to their homes. The museum had been vandalized, and the Sacred Heart Roman Catholic Church, the activists' original headquarters, was daubed with graffiti and militant slogans."[50]

Writer Desmond Smith credits AIM with capitalizing on the entire communications process:

> "...[With the] impact and immediacy of global communications, it is now possible for a small group of people to intimidate the strongest of governments....the techniques of TV and press take-over are in their infancy, but we may be sure that wherever the obsessed are gathered there are such

thoughts. To put an end to the collective penaliza-
tion of innocent people is a priority for the government and electorate alike. At the present time
newsmen are helpless victims in the adventurist
game of media blackmail."[51]

In the aftermath of the Wounded Knee occupation,
over 200 Oglala Indians and AIM members were indict-
ed on various counts.[52] The political forum shifted to the
courts, which were required to deal with the outcome of
the conflict as though it were a criminal matter only.

Although activists were restricted in their movement because of court involvement, the American Indian
Movement continued on at least two fronts. The more
subtle, theological dimension has been all but neglected in
media coverage, or in some cases treated with suspicion or
ridicule. The Indians may have destroyed those things at
Wounded Knee they believed were the result of the white
man's culture but they left their own heritage untouched –
graves from the 1890 massacre. There was little reference
to the fact that the Ghost Dance occurred at Wounded
Knee in 1973. In Vine Deloria's article in the *Christian Century* he speaks of the Ghost Dance:

> "The white man will kill his opposition rather than
> win it over by example or reasoning. There was
> Ghost Dancing at Wounded Knee in 1890 and also
> in 1973, but in neither case did it stop the marshal's
> bullets."[53]

In late 1973, the Mohawk newspaper, *Akwesasne Notes*,
published a letter from Russell Means, written while he

was in jail. Parts of the letter refer to the religious aspects of the movement:

"While I sit here in solitude in the white man's prison, I feel very strongly the Spirit. It is a good and wonderful experience. It was the same in Wounded Knee when we danced the Ghost Dance again."[54]

While the religious convictions penetrated the movement, the overt activities of AIM continued in a more or less organized manner. In particular, the managerial abilities of Douglass Durham, working for the Des Moines, Iowa, office of AIM for two years after the Occupation of Wounded Knee, Would become the subject of much discussion. The following chapter will explore his role in AIM – and his co-commitment to the FBI.

VII

TESTIMONY OF DOUGLASS DURHAM, FBI OPERATIVE

On March 13, 1975, Douglass Durham publicly admitted having acted as a paid operative of the Federal Bureau of Investigation (FBI) for almost two years, while he was working his way up to the top administrative post in the American Indian Movement (AIM). On April 6, 1976, Durham gave testimony, regarding the activities of AIM, before the Internal Security Subcommittee of the Senate Committee on the Judiciary.

Durham made his initial contact with AIM when he went into Wounded Knee on March 20, 1973. His entry into the area was arranged by the FBI and he posed as a photographer for *Pax*, a now defunct underground newspaper. For the next two years he was paid an average of $1,000 a month as he filed regular reports on plans and activities of AIM as an FBI operative.[1]

Durham's dual role raises two questions. One, what are the implications of an FBI operative posing as a repre-

sentative of a news medium? Two, how much did his presence within AIM alter its course or direction?

Durham was employed as a policeman in Des Moines,
Iowa, until 1964, at which time he went into his own business. Later, he returned as a paid intelligence agent of the
chief of police, operating in various cities on an exchange
program. Several of the Des Moines investigations paral-
leled those of the FBI. He was also a professional photographer, and had been asked by *Pax* to submit photos several months before Wounded Knee.

When the Wounded Knee assignment came up,
Durham found out that only major media representatives
were being given entrance. He contacted an FBI agent and
entry was arranged, along with an agreement to return to
them with photos and information.[2]

The matter of journalists accepting payment for
"volunteered" information and/or police or other intelligence gathering agents posing as journalists has come under heavy criticism from the Twentieth Century Fund. In
their 1972 report, *Press Freedoms Under Pressure*, reference is
made to the frequency of such practices raising "barriers
of suspicion that have made it more difficult for the press
to cover many events," and fourteen specific incidents are
cited, a few of them are:

- Siagon, 1969, two U.S. agents infiltrate the
  press corps.
- Army intelligence agents pose as TV camera-
  men during 1969 Presidential Inauguration
  in Washington, D.C.
- Two plainclothes officers pose as photographers for a weekly newspaper and photograph

Nassau County, New York, audience attending anti-war rally.

- General Motors stockholders' meeting covered by a Detroit policeman posing as a news photographer.
- FBI agents using TV cameras and tape recorders to interview demonstrators at a draft card burning demonstration in 1968.[3]

The Twentieth Century Fund Task Force condemns the practice of police, FBI agents and Army personnel masquerading as journalists because it "endangers the integrity of the press and renders it less effective in performing its responsibilities to society."[4]

New York City, Chicago, Detroit, and the District of Columbia police forces have issued orders condemning the practice of posing as journalists. FBI Director J. Edgar Hoover's response in writing to the task force in 1971 said that, "FBI agents are not permitted to pose as reporters or press photographers in the course of their investigation."[5] If that rule still held in 1973, then apparently it did not extend to the use of paid operatives in the case of Douglass Durham.

The task force's concern over the financial compensation to journalists for providing information drew this response from former Director Hoover:

The FBI accepts from any person information which may be of value in the course of an FBI investigation. The FBI does not now, and never has, actively recruited journalists as informants. However, there is no policy against accepting informa-

tion from a journalist or any news media representative if it is volunteered, which was the case with
Mr. Louis Salzberg and Mr. Carl Gilman. Both of
these individuals furnished information to the FBI
on a voluntary basis. They were paid for their services and expenses."[6]

The task force had difficulty reconciling the word
"volunteer" with being paid for services and expenses:

"When journalists are paid for providing information to the FBI or any other law enforcement agency, the result is an infiltration – and sullying – of the
profession."[7]

In the case of Douglass Durham it is difficult to assess which role he was involved in when he went to the
FBI agent for the purpose of gaining access to Wounded
Knee. His testimony before the Senate Subcommittee investigating internal security indicates he was already actively engaged as a professional news photographer, and as
an intelligence agent.

The second question previously posed regarding the
course that AIM may have taken had Durham not been
involved will have to give way to speculation. He brought
numerous skills with him when he began "working" for
AIM. Durham is a licensed pilot (4,000 hours logged), a
professional photographer, an electronics expert, a spe-
cialist in locking devices, an accomplished scuba diver,
expert marksman, experienced in business management,
and a theatrical make-up artist.[8]

Durham furnished the FBI with a complete set of the pictures he took inside AIM's defense perimeter at Wounded Knee. The FBI agent contact suggested he take a set of the photos to Harvey Major, a local Indian activist, and try to work his way into the small AIM chapter in Des Moines. He issued an additional irresistible challenge: "If you really wanted to you could go clear to the top of the American Indian Movement." Durham later admitted, "I am susceptible to challenges."[9]

In less than a month Durham was vice-chairman of the Des Moines chapter of AIM and did, in fact, work his way up:

> "In ten months he was the national chief of security for the American Indian Movement and coordinator of the Wounded Knee Legal Defense/Offense office in St. Paul, Minnesota; he had also established and become the director of a new national office for AIM."[10]

If anyone wanted to see Dennis Banks or Russell Means they had to go through Durham, and he held strategic control over AIM's operations for eight-and-a-half months while Banks and Means were involved in a federal trial in St. Paul.[11]

Durham gathered other titles in AIM: Public relations director of the Des Moines chapter; National AIM pilot; personal bodyguard to Dennis Banks; international charge d'affaires; and he traveled around the United States with the leaders of the movement as a national figure.

While the Wounded Knee occupation was still in progress, Harvey Major, chairman of the Des Moines chapter of AIM, and Douglass Durham began making contacts with Des Moines area churches in a fund raising effort. Major decided to occupy the grounds of the First Church of the Open Bible, a headquarters for a small denomination holding property in the city. AIM made a financial demand of $50,000 from the church to pay for neglect of American Indians, requested assurance that there would be no civil actions, and a commitment that a meeting of the Des Moines clergy would be called. Ministers would be asked to pledge support for AIM programs to benefit American Indians.[12]

An article by John Adams, staff member of the United Methodist Church's Board of Church and Society, and National Council of Churches representative involved in many of the contacts and negotiations concerning AIM, credits Durham with authorizing the list of sixteen demands presented to the church, and with becoming primary liaison with the church. Durham presented AIM's program to the clergy and proposed they pledge $33,000 a year. The clergy supported the proposal.[13]

When the Iowa annual conference of the United Methodist Church met in Des Moines in June of 1973, the Indians again occupied the grounds. They requested $150,000 in bail funds for Dennis Banks, national executive director of AIM – indicted by a federal grand jury for his activities at Wounded Knee. Harvey Major said that Banks was in hiding for fear of his life and because the bail was excessive. Durham made the major presentation before the church council on finance and administration, and according to those who attended he presented strong moral arguments, even quoting scripture.[14]

The clergy voted 564 to 429, following ninety minutes of debate, to provide $85,000 of the bail for Banks.[15] Durham's position in AIM was enhanced, and the movement's ambitions for coercing for large sums of money increased. In Durham's testimony before the Senate subcommittee in 1975, he indicated that they (AIM) pursued their demands in the two above mentioned incidents and in others because they believed they had the support and coverage of the press.[16]

Durham first met Dennis Banks in August of 1973, prior to the Sun Dance ceremony in Green Grass, South Dakota. Durham traveled with Harvey Major to the location to receive Bank's personal thanks for their fund raising effort. Banks became fascinated with Durham's photographs and asked him to take more pictures, and also showed interest in Durham's piloting ability. Their second meeting would take place following Durham's involvement and subsequent "arrest" in the Grimes State Office Building seizure in Des Moines.[17]

The Grimes State Office Building incident was the result of Durham convincing Ron Petite that a kidnapping of the Governor would be counter productive and they should hold an armed press conference in the office building instead. Durham described an armed press conference:

> "That would be to portray to the public an armed occupation to gain more press coverage for the American Indian Movement, stand up with rifles and bullets and say you are preparing to die for the occupation of the building until your demands are met."[18]

Durham took credit for maintaining a peaceful occupation, and when the ten AIM members surrendered after three hours his bond was paid by a bonding division of the pretrial release, court service program in Des Moines. The hundred dollar fine was paid by the Bureau of Criminal Investigation, and the record of his arrest was eradicated.[19] Durham had proved to AIM that he was capable of conducting an occupation. The basic goal was accomplished, publicity for AIM. Durham said:

> "Every type of media available came up, and did TV and newspaper interviews; it was a front-page story. It was carried by Associated Press and UPI coast to coast."[20]

Dennis Banks arrived in Des Moines after the occupation had ended. Durham said that Banks' purpose in being there was to create an impression that he was the peacemaker:

> "...the peace-bringing mediator who would solve these types of problems, if needed, in any future situation. It was a program and plan that I saw used and employed by Banks throughout the rest of my tenure with the American Indian Movement. The newspapers portrayed Banks then as the peacemaker, a reasonable, peace-loving man."[21]

After the Grimes State Office Building occupation, Durham and Banks began working closely. Banks was scheduled to appear in South Dakota in federal court on October 4, 1973, in connection with the Custer County

Court House protest charges. He couldn't be reached through intermediaries where he was hiding in northwest Canada. With the realization that the Iowa Methodists' $85,000 could be lost and jeopardize the whole movement, Durham rented a float plane and flew into the far north to locate Banks. Before Durham left he had arranged for a delay in the court appearance – and they returned hours before the scheduled appearance. Banks walked quietly into the court with his attorney and Douglass Durham. Banks was arrested, arraigned, and released on bail to appear in court the next day.[22]

Durham's involvement with AIM, the manner in which funds were raised and disbursed; plans for future militant action; links with revolutionary type organizations in foreign countries; support from "extremist domestic groups," such as the underground, socialist and communist newspapers is detailed in the two reports released by the Senate subcommittee in 1976. The subcommittee report, based on Durham's testimony, summarized its findings in nine categories:

1. The True dimensions of AIM – indicating that AIM does not speak for the majority of American Indians.
2. AIM as a Revolutionary Organization – frankly labeling the movement as revolutionary and committed to violence, and linking AIM leaders with the Marxist-Leninist philosophy.
3. Foreign ties – ties with Cuba, China, IRA (Irish Republican Army), Palestine Liberation Organization (PLO),

4. Domestic Extremist Ties – contacts with Weather Underground, the Communist Party, the Trotskyites, the Symbionese Liberation Army, the Black Panther Party, Youth Against War and Fascism, the Indo-China Solidarity Committee, and the Prisoners Solidarity Committee.

5. AIM and the Media – spectacular action resulted in massive coverage, often sympathetic – converting widespread sympathy for Indians into sympathy for AIM. The mass of media coverage fostered public opinion that AIM speaks for all Indians. A lack of seeking out views of tribal leaders and other legitimate Indian leaders.

6. Support from Federal, Church and Other sources – taking advantage of public relations build-up in media, AIM was able to obtain hundreds of thousands of dollars worth of support from government and religious sources.

7. Financial abuses – government funds given to AIM were used to perpetuate radical activities rather than to improve the lot of the American Indians.

8. Undercutting of legally constituted Indian authority – When government officials dealt with AIM and yielded to demands they undercut established authority.

9. The case of Judge Nichol – dealing with the "pre-judicial attitude" of the Federal judge who dismissed charges against Dennis Banks and Russell Means.[23]

Alert the Media

As part of Durham's testimony and documentation he presented the subcommittee with a copy of "The Operational Goals of National AIM" given him in confidence by Dennis Banks in October of 1974.[24] Section 8.0 of that document deals with media relations and is worth quoting for the purpose of understanding how a mass movement uses mass media:

> **MEDIA RELATIONS**
> Perhaps the most important element in AIM operations will be media relations. This function logically lies in AIM central, however, local chapters must participate at the 'grass roots' level. AIM must create the post of 'press secretary, minister of propaganda' or whatever is deemed suitable. The role of this single point will be the dissemination of information to the press which includes foreign and domestic outlets.
>
> The press secretary should accomplish the following initial tasks:
>
> A)   Conduct a national and world wide inventory of media outlets so as to develop a master index of all valid media contacts.
> B)   Differentiate this master index into national, international and local outlets.
> C)   Assign local outlets to local AIM chapters.
> D)   Develop the necessary machinery, equipment and procedures to affect a national and international press release or conference.

Marilyn Catherine McDonald MA

E)   Develop the necessary capability to prepare
     video tape coverage of AIM events and other
     activities for release to key media outlets.
F)   Create the image, in the media, that will be
     determined by the national leadership coun-
     cil or board.

The media function within AIM national will also
regulate the flow of communications to all chapters as well as outside agencies or other groups. The
media function shall be responsible to create "How
To" books for local chapters so that they too can
learn to use the media as a basic tool.[25]

Maintaining a media image was obviously an important movement strategy. But, while AIM struggled to get
their image before the public, competing with fast-break-
ing news stories of each day, they were being torn apart by
internal conflict and court appearances. Suspicions about
FBI and CIA infiltration ran high in August of 1973, when
AIM leader Carter Camp shot AIM director Clyde Bellecourt in the abdomen. Meanwhile, Durham inched his
way into top positions, apparently without anyone challenging him or suspecting his FBI ties. When Durham
revealed his assignment to infiltrate AIM he told Dennis
Banks and Vernon Bellecourt that his instructions had
been to "protect the life of Dennis Banks and enhance the
credibility of the American Indian Movement."[26]
    Durham's testimony in a closed-doors session before
the Senate Internal Security Subcommittee was made
public September 19, 1976. At that time, a Canadian government prosecutor responded to a portion of the report

by saying "it gave an exaggerated picture of the movement of Indian fugitives and arms across the U.S.-Canadian border."[27]

American Indian Movement leader Vernon Bellecourt characterized the subcommittee's description of AIM as a revolutionary organization as an attempt on the part of the FBI to "discredit the movement," and labeled it a disruptive tactic by the FBI. Bellecourt also said AIM has exposed Durham as a "pathological liar."[28]

In Portland, Oregon, local Indian leader John Talley, who had previously been associated with AIM work, expressed the opinion that the subcommittee's reference to AIM as revolutionary was true to the extent that a revolutionary is a person who seeks change. He added that at that time (September 20, 1976) the local AIM organization was inactive, although there were people who considered themselves AIM supporters.[29]

Lowell Curley, head of the Portland Urban Indian Council, said at the time that although AIM's work had not always been supported by every Indian organization in the country, "no Indian can discredit what AIM accomplished in focusing worldwide attention on Indian problems that continue to exist."[30]

Charlie Johnson, a former director of the Portland Urban Indian Center, said at the time the report was made public:

> "I would have been disappointed if the subcommittee's report, prompted by the FBI, would be anything but what it was. Any time a minority wishes to express some sort of self-determination, the FBI

Marilyn Catherine McDonald MA

> and other conservative groups are going to call it
> revolutionary and associated with Communists.
> All you have to do is look at how the FBI reacted to
> the work of Martin Luther King."[31]

Douglass Durham's Senate revelations about AIM raised protest from the National Council of Churches. Members of the NCC had been involved in negotiations in what they considered the interest of social justice. The churches objected to the fact that their activities were monitored along with AIM and considered it a breach of the first amendment because the FBI had "infiltrated the American Indian Movement and the United Methodist Church and other church bodies as well."[32]

At the 1975 meeting of the National Council of Churches in Chicago, the governing board passed a resolution calling upon NCC member churches to "seek disclosure under the Freedom of Information Act of any surveillance or improper activities by any federal agency against any of them, their members, or employees." The resolution states that such infiltration violates the "right to privacy, the freedom of association, and the freedom of religion."[33]

Durham, himself, expressed some concern regarding the matter of infiltration and surveillance after his experience with the FBI and AIM:

> "When you start looking for potential criminal
> activities and engage an undercover agent to be on
> the lookout for this, and in the course of reporting,
> report everything, what you're doing is saying that
> every citizen in the United States escapes the pos-

sibility of being a subject of surveillance. If movement groups are infiltrated because they have the potential for committing crimes, then it is only a small step to the full invasion of any citizen's privacy, for every individual has the potential for committing a crime."[34]

The FBI was very much involved in the surveillance of AIM activities over a considerable time. This involvement resulted in several confrontations. The following chapter will consider some of that involvement, the results of AIM leaders' court cases, and particularly follows Dennis Banks' hearings and extradition considerations in Oregon.

VIII

DENNIS BANKS IN OREGON

The publicized activities of mass movement leaders and supporters inevitably wane. And, it takes time for journalistic investigations to unravel the circumstances of the events. An account of a "Shootout at Pine Ridge" in July of 1975 appeared in *Time Magazine* at the time of the incident. Several months later the *Oregon Times* treated the same report in another way. Excerpts from the *Time Magazine* article follow:

"This time the victims were two FBI agents slaughtered by a band of Indian militants, and one of their attackers....four Indians kidnapped two young whites, released them a few hours later....two days later the FBI arrested one Indian and the following day sent agents Jack Coler and Ronald Williams, both 28, to Oglala with warrants for the arrest of the other three....the Indians apparently opened fire on the car when it reached a 20-foot high rocky bank. The agents radioed a May Day call and turned the car around but couldn't get away. The assailants apparently dragged the men from the car, stripped and shot them in the back of the head. More FBI agents and BIA police arrived and exchanged gunfire for several hours with some 16 Indians, killing one."[1]

Marilyn Catherine McDonald MA

Several months later this information appeared in the *Oregon Times* article, "The Government's Secret War Against the Indian:"

> "The first we heard of the shootout was this UPI release: 'Oglala, S.D. – Two FBI agents were ambushed and killed with repeated blasts of gunfire Thursday in an outbreak of bloodshed appearing to stem from the 1973 occupation of Wounded Knee.' This inflammatory and inaccurate message was, in fact, not written by UPI but by the FBI. Reporters were not permitted to verify the account. They were denied access to autopsy reports and to the scene itself. Thanks to the snooping of Joel Weisman for *Columbia Journalism Review*, we now know that the incident was not an 'ambush' but the spontaneous product of mutual fears. The agents were not 'dragged' from the car, 'stripped' and 'executed,' nor were the Indians hiding in 'sophisticated bunkers.'"[2]

Oregon Times identifies the apparent distortions of reality as resembling press manipulation methods described in the government's "Operation Cable Splicer" papers:

> "The 'Control Force-Media Relations' lesson calls for the creation of a central press center, such as that set up in this instance by the FBI's chief PR man, Tom Coll. All news releases must be 'coordinated' by this center in order to avoid 'distorted or unfavorable publicity' and in order that military actions 'be presented in an affirmative light.' The lesson also counsels that reporters' freedom of movement may be restricted 'when necessary.'"[3]

Leonard Peltier, a thirty-two year old Sioux from Grand Forks, North Dakota, fled to Canada when he was sought in connection with the death of the two FBI agents. While he was in a Canadian jail fighting extradition an organization called Amnesty International sent a letter to Justice Minister Ron Basford, stating that Peltier might be in danger if he were returned. He said that information gathered by the organization indicated a "pattern of deliberate attempts by the FBI to persecute, harass and render impotent the leadership of the American Indian Movement."[4]

Two years after the shootout incident, Leonard Peltier was sentenced to two consecutive life terms (June 1977) in a Fargo, North Dakota, court. He did not receive a death penalty because that had been waived in extraditing him from Canada.[5]

At the beginning of 1976 Russell Means had spent twelve out of twenty-four months in court and still faced another eight or so of trials.[6] Means accused the FBI of provoking incidents in which he became involved. He named FBI agent Howard John Fuller as being "involved in three out of the last four times I've been shot."[7] At the time of the Yanktown Sioux reservation shooting that placed Means in the hospital with a .22-caliber gunshot wound in the abdomen he accused the press of obscuring the real situation. He claimed they were exaggerating a feud between himself and Dennis Banks, and reporting dissension that did not exist.[8]

In August of 1976, Means was acquitted by the Circuit Court jury of a charge of murder in a 1975 barroom killing. The verdict came after a three-day trial and twenty hours of jury deliberation. Means still had to face trials on charges of assault at McLaughlin, S.D., and riot and assault in the disturbance at Custer, S.D., in 1973. Charges of assault, larceny, and conspiracy in connection with the 1973 Wounded Knee occupation were dismissed.[9]

Although AIM's national offices were located in Minnesota the movement traveled with the leadership, and the court trials. In April of 1976, *The Oregonian* headlined an article by Wayne Thompson, "Banks trial may make Portland AIM's big target." Speculation that Portland would become central to AIM's activity stemmed from a combination of factors: the national media spotlight was on Oregon during the Oregon Presidential primary campaign; Dennis Banks was building up support in his fight against extradition to South Dakota; Banks made public statements that he planned to launch his program from the west coast, "...from what I've seen so far, I would like to stay and carry out AIM's national programs from here and from California."[10]

Banks was scheduled to go to trial May 12, along with Kenneth Moses Loud Hawk, Russ James Redner and Ka-Mook Banks, Dennis Banks' wife. The four were charged with several counts of illegal possession of firearms stemming from a November 14, 1975, incident near Ontario, Oregon, when state police stopped two vehicles and allegedly discovered the firearms and explosives.[11] Dennis Banks apparently fled the scene but was later returned to Oregon from California. Redner and Loud Hawk were charged with a class "C" felony and bail was set at $50,000 each. Usual bail for class "C" felonies is $1,500.

KaMook was sent to Wichita, Kansas, to face a fire-arms charge stemming from the explosion of a vehicle in which she was traveling with seven other persons on September 10, 1975. Occupants of the vehicle escaped unin-jured but KaMook was charged with possession of World War II hand-grenades which were in the vehicle and did not explode.[12] She gave birth to her second daughter while under twenty-four hour security in Kansas. The infant was named "Iron Door Woman" signifying the time already spent in jail. Wichita set bail at $20,000 for KaMook and returned her to Portland to stand trial with the others connected with the Ontario incident.[13] In September of 1976, KaMook stood trial in Wichita and was placed on three years probation after pleading guilty to the firearms and explosives charge in that state.[14]

While the four AIM members awaited trial in Port-land they organized community support with rallies, fundraisers, and press conferences. In January, $1,400 was raised when a meeting was held in the northwest Portland home shared by Jack and Micki Scott and Portland Trail Blazer basketball player Bill Walton. AIM leaders also launched a petition drive for signatures to be presented to Gov. Bob Straub to deny the extradition of Banks to South Dakota, where he was wanted for sentencing on a convic-tion resulting from a clash between law enforcement of-ficers and AIM leaders.[15]

The following newspaper headlines and excerpts tell the Dennis Banks in Oregon story, for the most part:

Marilyn Catherine McDonald MA

Banks Seeks Oregon Sanctuary
Eugene – American Indian Movement leader Dennis Banks told University of Oregon students Thursday he hope Oregon will be the first of many states to refuse to extradite him to South Dakota.[16]

Oregon Journal, April 23, 1976

Prosecution Delay Bid Rejected in AIM Trial
The 9th U.S. Circuit Court of Appeals in San Francisco has denied a request by U.S. Attorney Sidney I. Lezak of Oregon for postponement of a May 12 trial date for four American Indian Movement (AIM) members on firearms and explosives charges.

Lezak said Tuesday the ruling may result in dismissal of the case, but that the government will stand by its decision not to go to trial without an appeals court ruling on dynamite evidence which a federal judge in Portland has banned from use at trial.

U.S. District Judge Robert C. Belloni, on March 10, suppressed the dynamite as evidence, holding that seven cases of the explosive allegedly seized from two vehicles near Ontario last Nov. 14, were improperly disposed of by police.[17]

The Oregonian, April 28, 1976

Methodists Hear Banks' Flee Story
Dennis Banks, an American Indian who has asked Gov. Bob Straub not to extradite him to South Dakota, was given a forum Tuesday by Methodist leaders who support Banks' attempt to stay in Oregon.

Methodists held a press conference for Banks at the Memorial Coliseum Tuesday where their General Conference is being held.[18]

Oregon Journal, May 4, 1976

Dismissal Seen in Banks Charge
Assistant U.S. Attorney Bill Youngman said charges against Banks and three other American Indian Movement members probably will be dismissed next week.[19]

Oregon Journal, May 4, 1976

Indians Plead for End to Injustice
American Indians were joined by nearly 300 persons Saturday in an enthusiastic demonstration calling for an end to injustices against Indians and for a system that will 'serve the people.'[20]

The Oregonian, May 9, 1976

Delay in Banks Trial Sought
The government on Wednesday will ask U.S. District Court Judge Robert Belloni to reconsider his denial of the government's motion to postpone the trial of Dennis Banks and three other American Indians.[21]

Oregon Journal, May 11, 1976

Lezak Denies Claim That Banks Trial Stalled
Sidney I. Lezak, U.S. Attorney for Oregon, denied flatly Tuesday that the government has sought to delay for political purposes the trial...
'the cold fact of the matter,' Lezak said in a memorandum filed in the U.S. District Court in Portland, 'is that defendants have repeatedly sought continu-

ances of the trial while engaging in a concentrated effort to gain public sympathy by misstating the record and the government's position with respect to the trial of this case. Accordingly, their efforts in this regard must be made a matter of public record.'

The memorandum states that the court has held no further delay of the trial for the defendants is justified under the Speedy Trial Act. Lezak contends, however that a 'pragmatic reading of the act' does not support trial without evidence which is the subject of an appeal.[22]

The Oregonian, May 12, 1976

U.S. Judge Throws Out Banks Case

American Indian Movement leader Dennis Banks, 39, and three other federal Indian defendants were freed of explosive and firearms charges Wednesday by U.S. District Court Judge Robert C. Belloni.

Defendants, their lawyers and supporters, many clad in traditional brightly colored Indian garb, embraced and shouted as the judge closed the short hearing.

Spectators in the Overflowing courtroom then filed out as Banks announced a victory conference outside the Courthouse.

...Belloni said he did not want to dismiss the case without trial, but that 'for some reason I do not understand, the government is not ready.'[23]

Oregon Journal, May 12, 1976

Banks Expects Reindictment

Standing on the steps of the U.S. Courthouse, Dennis Banks, American Indian Movement leader, held up his daughter Ta Tiopa Maza Win (Iron Door Woman), 4 months old.

'She was born behind bars in Wichita, Kan.; born to go forward to tell the truth about how it is to be born behind bars. The action today is going to open some of those (barred) doors,' Banks shouted to a crowd of newsmen and well-wishing followers after Wednesday's dismissal of federal firearms charges...

The AIM leader said he expected the federal government to attempt pressing re-indictments growing out of the Nov. 14, 1975, incident near Ontario...

'We are convinced that the prosecution of the Indian people will continue,' he (Banks) said.[24]

The Oregonian, May 13, 1976

Judge Sets Banks' Bail at $10,000

Circuit Court Judge Patrick Dooley Thursday raised the bail amount for American Indian leader Dennis Banks from $5,000 to $10,000.

The amount means that Banks must post a 10 percent security amount of $500 to remain on release while his extradition to South Dakota is considered....

Dooley said that bail should be set in an amount equal to that which Banks forfeited in South Dakota.

The request was made by Deputy District Attorney David Hattrick, who said he was speaking for South Dakota authorities.

Banks fled from South Dakota after conviction and before sentencing on charges of armed rioting and assault. In doing so, he forfeited the $10,000 put up by two Methodist Church agencies....

Banks argued before Judge Dooley that he is not likely to flee from Oregon because he wants to stay in this state.[25]

Oregon Journal, May 13, 1976

U.S. Still Hopes to Try Banks on Explosive Rap

The Portland U.S. attorney's office does not consider the dismissal of charges against four American Indians Wednesday the end of the line for prosecution of the case.[26]

Oregon Journal, May 13, 1976

Straub Asks Banks Defense

Gov. Bob Straub has asked lawyers involved in the case to send him written arguments on whether he should send Dennis Banks....back to South Dakota....

The governor said he will seek to make public his decision by June 7 unless lawyers need more time.[27]

Oregon Journal, May 18, 1976

Banks in California
Straub Drops AIM Extradition Case

...Straub said friends of Banks advised him informally that Banks would remain in California, where Gov. Edmund G. (Jerry) Brown Jr. also has extradition papers from South Dakota before him.

...The governor said Banks' predicament has stimulated more mail than any other issue he has encountered as the state's chief executive. Sullivan (Straub's legal council) estimated the governor has received

500 letters from Oregonians and more than 2,000 from Californians – most against extradition.[29]

The Oregonian, June 10, 1976

Judge Grants Straub Delay on Banks

...Dooley said that although one of his options Tuesday would have been to dismiss the fugitive case against Banks in Oregon, he believed such action was 'inappropriate' because, in his opinion, 'the governor's failure to act was based on inaccurate legal advice.'[30]

The Oregonian, 16, 1976

Banks Wins 30-Day Delay

Circuit Court Judge Pat Dooley Tuesday reset the date of the extradition warrant hearing for....Banks to July 15 because Banks has been jailed in California....

On Monday, Banks was taken into custody after he told a San Francisco Municipal Court Judge that he had not been able to raise an additional $5,000 bail set a week earlier....

Roberts (Banks attorney) said that Banks' supporters are attempting to raise the entire $5,000 required to release him. California, which is on the bail bond system requires posting the stated amount of bail, unlike Oregon, which requires a 10 percent security amount.[31]

Oregon Journal, June 15, 1976

Banks Out on Bond

...Banks, who failed to appear at a hearing on South Dakota's extradition request in Portland Tuesday because he was in jail, has been freed on $500 cash bond in San Francisco.

...Roberts said he had won a ruling to reduce the Indian leader's bond from $5,000 to the lesser amount from San Francisco Municipal Judge Mary Pajalich.[32]

The Oregonian, June 17, 1976

New Banks Date Sought

The date of Dennis Banks' next extradition hearing should be moved up, now that he has been released from jail in San Francisco, Multnomah County District Attorney Davit Hattrick said Thursday.[33]

Oregon Journal, June 17, 1976

Straub Extradition Decision Promised

If Gov. Bob Straub has not made a decision on South Dakota's request for extradition of....Banks by July 2...Dooley will dismiss the fugitive complaint....

In making the statement about dismissal, Dooley declared, ' I do not in any sense presume to tell the governor of this state what his actions should be or that he should act at all...But this is the last time I'm going to hear this case.'[34]

Oregon Journal, June 22, 1976

Banks Complaint Dismissed; Warrant Ordered

Dennis Banks is no longer wanted as a fugitive in the state of Oregon, but the same judge who dismissed that complaint against Banks also ordered that a warrant be prepared for the Indian leader's arrest for his failure to appear in court Friday in Portland.

...Dooley, saying he felt like a Ping-Pong ball in the long-running Banks case...

Dooley, acting on his own motion, also ordered that Banks forfeit $1,000 security amount for bail in the case....

Haas [Dist. Atty.] said he was looking into the possibility of charging Banks with failure to appear, a felony punishable by up to five years in prision.[35]

The Oregonian, July 3, 1976

Hearing for Banks Postponed

San Francisco (UPI) – A judge on Thursday reduced bail for...Banks to $2,500 and postponed until Nov. 15 a hearing on whether he will be extradited to South Dakota to face armed riot and assault charges.

Municipal Judge Mary Moran Pajalich said she was informed Monday by the office of California Gov. Edmund G. Brown, Jr. that he has been busy with legislative matters and had not yet acted on an extradition warrant from South Dakota....

'Brown hasn't indicated anything one way of the other,' Banks said before the hearing. 'I'm not disappointed. He could have sent me back already.'[36]

Oregon Journal, September 16, 1976

S.D. Wins Court Test for Banks

Sacramento, Calif. (AP) – A state appeals court Monday ordered Gov. Edmund Brown Jr. to extradite American Indian Movement leader Dennis Banks to South Dakota on a warrant stemming from a riot-assault conviction.

...Brown's legal affairs secretary, J. Anthony Kline, said he would urge an appeal of the ruling, which

he said was unprecedented, to the state Supreme
Court.

...Brown's office fought South Dakota's request
for extradition, arguing it was studying allegations
that Banks' life would be in danger if he returned
to South Dakota.

Banks location was not immediately known.

Banks could fight the extradition warrant after an
arrest.[37]

The Oregonian, April 26, 1977

Newsmakers and participants do not function entirely free of the influence of the media that reports their
activity. Movement leaders, like Dennis Banks, constantly
reassess their image in light of what is said about them,
and often they reshape that image. Judges, potential ju-
rors, and attorneys are aware of the presence of media representatives and of media reports of their actions and the
circumstances in which they operate.

Newsmakers and participants perceive their roles
individually and differently. A representative of the U.S.
Marshals office in the Federal Court House in Portland, a
few days prior to the May 12, 1976, Dennis Banks hearing,
admitted that he rarely read the reports concerning cases;
"I don't read what goes into the press. It seems awful different from what's said up there."[38] The U.S. Marshals office had the responsibility of deciding who would be allowed into the court room.

On the morning of the hearing, crowds jammed the
hallway outside Judge Belloni's court. It was impossible to
get anywhere near the doors, so I went back to the main
floor and took the elevator, which let me off quite near the

courtroom doors. I had been told that media representatives had to take their chances on gaining entry. Bill Walton stood head and shoulders above the crowd and when the Marshals let the principals involved in the case enter, Walton was admitted along with the family.

Reporters were permitted entrance, subject to credentials, and one reporter-artist team from each of the local papers. I gained entry based on verification of my membership in the National Federation of Press Women, and said I was working on my masters thesis which concerned this hearing. Media representatives were seated in the jury box since it would be empty, and I sat next to a reporter for the *Peoples World* from Berkeley, California.

There were few spectators in the court, aside from the media representatives. It is difficult for an observer to determine how much of the activity in the courtroom is a show for the media and how much of it is spontaneous. The defendants and their attorneys stood around the Counsel table and were led in prayer by Ellen Moves Camp before the proceedings began. The Indian prayer brought responses from supporters in the courtroom. A baby, Dennis Banks' baby, cried. A toddler wandered freely about the courtroom during the proceedings. Judge Belloni rendered his decision to the beating of drums and Indian whooping and howling.

Dennis Banks, accompanied by red-shirted AIM security men with the upside-down American flags on their sleeves, held a "victory" news conference on the steps of the courthouse. Drum beating and chanting continued in the background and clenched fist victory salutes punctuated remarks by Banks and his attorney Dennis Roberts.

Roberts drew supporters' cheers when he applauded their efforts in being able to "kick the Government in the ass," and Banks remarked that the federal government would "try some 'tricky dicky'" move against him in the future.

The courtroom atmosphere on June 15 was slightly different. After a considerable wait in the hall the room was opened on a first-come, first-serve basis, and again media persons sat in the jury box. Circuit Court Judge Patrick Dooley's courtroom was smaller than that of Judge Bellonie, and AIM security personnel stood at the door to prevent others from entering once capacity was reached. When Dennis Banks entered the room a voice from the back said, "All rise," an order customarily reserved for the entry of the presiding judge. Banks calmly settled seating problems and directed his supporters who could not find seats that they would have to leave. While reporters were still in the hall waiting entry to the courtroom, I asked a local television newsman if he thought the media was being used in this particular coverage. He said, "Even if we are, we have to report what's happening." Editors and reporters are reluctant to omit coverage when the other papers or stations are on the scene.

At one point in the court proceedings Banks' attorney Roberts faced the members of the press in the jury box and said, "I'm not going to be as eloquent as Mr. Hattrick (Deputy District Attorney speaking for the state of South Dakota), but then I'm aware this is not a jury." A few minutes later Judge Patrick Dooley discussed the matter of extradition, "I have nothing to say about extradition.

I don't just go home and read a funny book. I read what's going on. I don't know if Dennis Banks' fears are founded or unfounded."

Legal entanglements have caused AIM leaders to scatter or become confined by the law. Local organizations have faltered and fallen apart. The once potent newsmakers and important news have become less so as time passes and competition for media time and space grows fierce.

IX
ALERT THE
MEDIA
CONCLUSION

A mass movement appears to die. The visible body of organization is in a weakened position in relation to its ability to command public attention or apply pressure on authorities. The underlying spirit of the movement may continue to grow, unnoticed, and produce favorable results. But, once the movement ceases to be a public attraction it has passed out of that phase that justifies calling it a "mass" movement. The primary difference lies in the lack of attention by the "mass" media.

The original thesis contained here presented considerable proof to demonstrate that the American Indian Movement, a twentieth century mass movement, depended almost entirely on media exposure to extend its dynamic phase of growth and development. The thesis contended that when AIM's media exposure diminished the "mass" part of the movement also diminished.

Media coverage of AIM diminished for several reasons:

Marilyn Catherine McDonald MA

1. AIM leaders were being restricted in their activities because of court involvement and the news they were making was less spectacular or interesting to journalists and editors.
2. The public tired of hearing or reading about the movement, and media representatives were sensitive to those feelings.
3. The competition for media time and space became a vital factor. AIM competed with news of Watergate, and Patricia Hearst.
4. AIM members and supporters could no longer sustain the effort required to keep a mass movement going. Personal responsibilities eventually draw participants away from a movement they have perceived as temporary.

American Indians, on and off the reservations, continue to struggle with the matter of defining their identity in relation to their culture and the American-way-of-life. Cultural changes continually take place. Some recapture and rebuild the past; others find ways of surviving or advancing by using the existing institutions and organizations. There seems little chance that there will be another major Indian movement with the dynamic impact of AIM for a considerable time. For, if what they advocate has any truth to it, they intend to see the white man destroy himself, and the Indian will then regain the land.

Their strength, if they have any remaining from the movement, is in their commitment to common goals. Even those Indians who objected to the methods of the movement have benefited from the recognition and renewed interest in Indian causes. How long that interest lasts remains to be seen. Some subtle unity must exist as a result of having shared some degree of success. Only the Indians know for certain who their heroes are.

In less than a decade the Indians have forced the media and the public to give additional attention to matters of water rights, fishing rights, law enforcement on and around the reservations, jurisdiction on the reservations, boundaries, treaties, self-determination and self-government, restitution, taxes, social service, resources and employment. AIM cannot take credit for all the achievements of the American Indians over the decade, but in some way the movement may have caused the authorities to react more favorably, in a pacifying way, to the Indian leaders and communities outside the influence of AIM to prevent borderline Indians from joining the movement.

AIM has created divisions within Indian communities, but it also reached many Indians in search of identity, particularly the young urban Indians. It will take time, perhaps in Indian time and not in the white man's time, to assess the effects of the AIM phenomenon on Indians and on the American society.

A newspaper article by Neal R. Peirce defines areas of conflict between whites and Indians on or near reservations in western America. He credits young Indian leaders with "speaking out and challenging states and counties that assert jurisdiction over Indian country." He summed up the relationship of movement toward change and the spirit of the people:

> "Their role [young leaders] is more important than the highly publicized American Indian Movement

(AIM), although AIM has helped create a psychological climate for greater Indian independence,
just as radical black power groups helped make the
demands of moderate black civil rights organizations seem more credible in the '60s".[1]

The purpose of the original thesis contained within
this book was to bring together bodies of data on the mass
movement, the mass media, and AIM – to lay groundwork
for future study of these types of interrelationships.

By introducing the profile of a Sioux Indian, Devere
East Man, in Chapter I, it was hoped that the reader would
find some human element that all people share in common
so that the following chapters of hard data would have
personal relevance. It was difficult finding proof that the
Ghost Dance was performed at Wounded Knee in 1973.
One comment by Vine Deloria in a periodical provided a
source, another mention occurred in the Mohawk newspaper, but the third statement of proof came from Devere
East Man. This proved an assumption made early in the
research that there definitely was an underlying spirituality in the American Indian Movement that the leaders
were perceived by the members as being charismatic. The
movement, in effect, proved to have strains of the messianic.

The chapter on mass movements provided criteria
by which to measure AIM. It gave a concise definition of
movement toward social change necessary in the forma-
tive stages of the thesis.

Chapter III presented some facts and definitions
of media power as a base for explaining how AIM incor-

porated that power into their arsenal of resources. Many changes occurred within media as a result of the heightened activity of the mass movements. Media personnel were forced to face the fact that their channels of communication were being abused in some cases. The Twentieth Century Fund study of government and press relationships was the forerunner of the National News Council. The council has eighteen members representative of newspaper editors, publishers and reporters, and those outside the field of journalism. The council meets every three months and considers itself the independent watchdog on press, radio and television. The council has existed since 1975 and former Congresswoman Edith Green serves as a member of the subcommittee on the free press. The other subcommittee is devoted to the investigation of complaints against the media.[2]

The information in Chapter III details the need for some kind of self-examination by the media, and the council met some of that need. It was not as well received by media in the beginning as it is at the present.

Chapter IV is a lengthy examination of Indian culture. It focuses primarily on the Plains Indian, specifically the Sioux, since AIM's major event was the occupation of Wounded Knee. The background in symbolic language, beliefs and customs is necessary in understanding the significance of Wounded Knee 1973. Understanding something about the culture enables the reader to understand why the AIM leaders found it necessary to go to the reservation traditionalists and spiritual leaders to learn the language of their people. At that point AIM took its definite turn toward the spiritual.

Chapter V explained how and why AIM came to be in relationship to the events and people of that time. Was the time right for such a movement? Indian spiritual leader Devere East Man believes the formation of the movement and the events were inevitable and prophetic.

Chapter VI dealt with the events at Wounded Knee in 1973 and points out the difficulties incurred by the media. At this time the preceding chapters should prove valuable points of reference.

Douglass Durham added an interesting aspect to AIM in particular, but also to mass movements in general. Chapter VII details the manner in which a paid FBI operative becomes a significant part of the movement and leaves the question open as to his influence and contribution, as well as the function and survival of the movement.

Chapter VIII was an attempt to examine primarily local newspaper reports of a series of events involving Dennis Banks' court battles in Oregon and California. The coverage of mass movement events and leaders in and out of the court room presents some problems for the journalist. The personal involvement of the thesis writer may serve as a clue in determining what the journalist brings to the assignment, and how that affects the results of the report.

———

One of the major problems encountered in the research at the time was finding books or periodicals dealing specifically with the American Indian Movement. (Much more has been written and is now available on a number of websites since the time this body of research was assembled.) *The Guide to Periodical Literature* proved to be the best source of information. Many more items were discarded than included in this study, and each inclusion was carefully weighed regarding its contribution to the original thesis work.

The original study can be expanded by consulting the newspaper files in other states, such as South Dakota, California, Minnesota, for articles about the American Indian Movement – and drawing comparisons.

Other mass movements now can be studied by using this work as a resource. Persons directly involved in AIM and in the media coverage of AIM events could be consulted to broaden this research, and to clarify issues.

Other journalists may find this study helpful in defining their particular areas of influence and responsibility in matters of mass movement coverage and reporting.

ALERT THE MEDIA ENDNOTES

Preface

1. Marshall McLuhan, *The Medium is the Massage* (United States and Canada: Bantam Books, Inc., 1967), p.8.

I. Introduction

1. Interview with Devere East Man "Papasan," spiritual leader for the Indians in the Portland, Oregon, area. A counselor for youth at the White Cloud Center, 14 October 1976.

II. Movement Toward Social Change

1. Gary T. Marx and James L. Wood, "Strands of Theory and Research in Collective Behavior," *Annual Review of Sociology* 1 (1975): p.375
2. Ibid.
3. Ibid., p.377.
4. Kenneth Burke, *Language as Symbolic Action* (Los Angeles: University of California Press, 1966), p.30.

5.   Alfred R. Lindesmith and Anselm L. Strauss, *Social Psychology* (New York: Holt, Rinehart and Winston, 1968), p.53.

6.   Ibid., p.55.

7.   Ibid.

8.   Carlos Castaneda, *Journey to Ixtlan* (New York: Pocket Books, 1975), p.viii-ix.

9.   Leland M. Griffin, "A Dramatistic Theory of the Rhetoric of Movements," *Critical Responses to Kenneth Burke*, ed. Wm. H. Rueckert, (Minnesota: University of Minnesota Press, 1969), p.462.

10. Ibid.

11. Ibid., p.456.

12. Marx and Wood, "Strands of Theory," p.369.

13. Griffin, "A Dramatistic Theory," p.463.

14. Lindesmith, *Social Psychology*, p.283.

15. Ibid., p.291.

16. Ibid., p.361.

17. Neil J. Smelser, *Theory of Collective Behavior* (New York: The Free Press of Glencoe, 1963), p.325.

18. William A. Gamson, *Power and Discontent* (Illinois: The Dorsey Press, 1968), p.40.

19. Smelser, *Theory of Collective Behavior*, p.313.

20. Marx and Wood, "Strands of Theory," p.408.

21. Smelser, *Theory of Collective Behavior*, p.327.

22. Marks and Wood, "Strands of Theory," p.412.

23. Ibid., p.413.

24. Griffin, "A Dramatistic Theory," p.461.

25. Marx and Wood, "Strands of Theory," p.397.

26. Burke, *Language Symbolic*, p.36.

27. Marx and Wood, "Strands of Theory," p.386

28. Ibid., p.397.
29. Smelser, *Theory of Collective Behavior*, p.355.
30. Lindesmith, *Social Psychology*, p.340.
31. Marx and Wood, "Strands of Theory," p.385.
32. Ibid., p.383.
33. Gamson, *Power and Discontent*, p.34.
34. Marx and Wood, "Strands of Theory," p.395.
35. Ibid., p.396.
36. Ibid., p.397.
37. Ibid.,
38. Lindesmit, *Social Psychology*, p.345.
39. Griffin, "Dramatistic Theory," p.464.
40. Jerome Skolnick, *The Politics of Protest: Violent Aspects of Protest and Confrontation*, Staff report to the National Commission on Causes and Prevention of Violence (New York: Simon and Schuster, 1969), p.11.
41. Skolnick, *Politics of Protest*, p.xiii.
42. Gamson, *Power and Discontent*, p.76.
43. Ibid., p.114.
44. Smelser, *Theory of Collective Behavior*, p.325.
45. Gamson, *Power and Discontent*, p.83.
46. Ibid., pp.98-99.
47. Marx and Wood, "Strands of Theory," p.387.
48. Gamson, *Power and Discontent*, pp.2-10.
49. Ibid., p.36.
50. Marx and Wood, "Strands of Theory," p.401.
51. Griffin, "Dramatistic Theory," p.465.
52. Gamson, *Power and Discontent*, p.112.
53. Ibid., p.116.
54. Ibid., p.137.
55. Skolnick, *Politics of Protest*, p.xiii.

56. Ibid., p.98.
57. Ibid., p.243.
58. Gamson, *Power and Discontent*, p.194.
59. *Marx and Wood,* "Strands of Theory," pp.415-416.

III. Mass Media – Power and Responsibility

1. Edward T. Hall, Ph.D., *The Silent Language* (Greenwich, Connecticut: Fawcett Publications, 1959), p.54.
2. Harold A. Innis, *The Bias of Communication* (Toronto: University of Toronto Press, 1951), p.33.
3. Hall, *Silent*, p.56.
4. Ibid., p.58.
5. Ibid., p.33.
6. Ibid., p.166.
7. Tamotsu Shibutani, *Improvised News* (New York: Bobbs-Merrill Co., 1966), p.21.
8. Innis, *Bias*, p.44.
9. Ibid., p.41.
10. Hall, *Silent*, p.74.
11. Ibid., p.20.
12. Jean-Louis Servan-Schreiber, *The Power to Inform, Media: The business of information* (New York: McGraw-Hill, 1974), p.193.
13. Ibid., p.1997.
14. Arthur M. Schlesinger, *Prelude to Independence: The Newspaper War on Britain 1764-1776* (New York: Alfred A. Knopf, 1958), p.33.
15. James Rowe, Chairman, *Press Freedoms Under Pressure: Report of the Twentieth Century Fund Task Force on the Government and the Press*, Background paper

by Fred P. Graham, (New York: Twentieth Century Fund, 1972), p.55.

16. Ibid., p.56

17. Ibid., p.59

18. Ibid.

19. Ibid.

20. Peter Lisagor, "From Triumph to Tragedy," *The World Book Year Book 1975* (Chicago: Field Enterprises Educational Corporation, 1975), pp.58-79.

21. Ibid.

22. Everette E. Dennis and William L. Rivers, *Other Voices: New Journalism in America* (San Francisco: Canfield Press, 1974), p.iii.

23. Martin H. Seiden, *Who Controls the Mass Media? Popular Myths and Economic Realities* (New York: Basic Books, Inc., 1974), p.150.

24. Robert Stein, *Media Power: Who is Shaping Your Picture of the World?* (Boston: Houghton Mifflin, 1972), p.53.

25. Shibutani, *Improvised News*, p.172.

26. Ibid., p.41.

27. Ibid., p.209.

28. Seiden, *Who Controls?*, p.223.

29. Leverett Richards, "Disclosure by TV Newsmen Urged," *Oregonian* (Portland), October 27 , 1976, p.C 8.

30. Ibid.

31. Stein, *Media Power*, p.260.

32. Ibid.

33. Servan-Schreiber, *Power to Inform*, p.143.

34. Ibid., p.203.

Marilyn Catherine McDonald MA

35. Stein, *Media Power*, p.261.
36. Servan-Schreiber, *Power to Inform*, p.205.
37. Joyce Gelb and Marian Lief Palley, *The Politics of Social Change* (New York: Holt, Rinehart and Winston, 1971), p. 494.
38. Ibid., pp.494-495.
39. Allen D. Grimshaw, *Racial Violence in the United States* (Chicago: Aldine Publishing Co., 1969), p.513.
40. Ibid.
41. Servan-Schreiber, *Power to Inform*, p.287.
42. Ibid., 147.
43. Ibid., p.117.
44. Ibid., pp.240-241.
45. Ibid., p.198.
46. Ibid., p.201.
47. Shibutani, *Improvised News*, p.148.
48. Ibid., p.164.
49. Ibid., p.209.
50. "Television news 'new kid on the block.'" *Press Woman*: Publication of the National Federation of Press Women, Inc., vol.39, no.11, November 1976, p.2.
51. Stein, *Media Power*, p.251.
52. Seiden, *Who Controls?* P.125.
53. Gelb and Palley, *Politics of Social Change*, p.495.
54. Ibid.,
55. Stein, *Media Power*, pp.243-244.
56. Ibid., p.246.
57. Grimshaw, *Racial Violence*, p.514.
58. Stein, *Media Power*, p.265.
59. Ibid., 253.
60. Ibid.

61. Ibid.
62. Ibid., p.41.

IV. American Indian Culture

1. Vine Deloria, Jr., *We Speak, You Listen* (New York: MacMillan Publishing Co., 1970), p.32.
2. Ibid., p.170.
3. Idem., "Religion and the Modern American Indian," *Current History*, December 1974, p.253.
4. Idem., *We Speak*, p.17.
5. Idem., *Custer Died for Your Sins* (New York: MacMillan Publishing Co., 1969), p.200.
6. Ibid., p.27.
7. Hyemeyohsts Storm, *Seven Arrows* (New York: Harper Row, 1972), p.212.
8. Ibid., pp.197-81.
9. Ibid., p.11.
10. Ibid., p.9-10.
11. Ibid., p.210.
12. Ben Sidran, *Black Talk* (New York: Harper Row Publishing Co., paperback, 1971), p.4.
13. John G. Neihardt, *Black Elk Speaks* (New York: William Morrow and Co., 1932), pp.198-99.
14. Storm, *Seven*, p.14.
15. Ibid., pp.14-20.
16. Ibid., p.20.
17. Ibid., pp.20-26.
18. Neihardt, *Black Elk*, passim.
19. Storm, *Seven*, passim.
20. Jimm G. Good Tracks, "Native American Noninterference," *Social Work* (November 1973): p.30.

21. Ibid., p.31.
22. Ibid.
23. Ibid., p.33.
24. Deloria, *Custer*, p.6.
25. David Humphreys Miller, *Ghost Dance* (New York: Duell, Sloan and Pierce,, 1959), p.20.
26. Deloria, *Custer*, p.6.
27. Storm, *Seven*, p.63.
28. Ibid., p.67.
29. Neihardt, *Black Elk*, p.147.
30. Ibid., p.234.
31. Ibid., 276.
32. Deloria, *Custer*, p.102.
33. Idem., "Religion Indian," p.102.
34. Dee Brown, *Bury My Heart at Wounded Knee* (New York: Holt, Rinehart and Winston, 1970), p.32.
35. Ibid., p.201.
36. Ibid., p.209.
37. Ibid., p.154.
38. Royal B. Hassick, *The Sioux: Life and Customs of a Warrior Society* (Norman: University of Oklahoma Press, 1964), p.226.
39. Deloria, "Religion Indian," p.250.
40. Ibid., p.251.
41. Storm, *Seven*, p.125.
42. Miller, *Ghost Dance*, p.vii.
43. Ibid., pp.243-245.
44. Ibid., p.244.
45. Ibid., p.276.
46. Brown, *Bury Heart*, p.312.
47. Ibid., p.441.

48. Deloria, *Custer*, p.22.
49. Miller, *Ghost Dance*, pp.14-15.
50. Ibid., p.295.
51. Ibid., p.57.
52. Ibid., p.24.
53. Ibid., pp.24-25.
54. Ibid.
55. Ibid.
56. Ibid., p.26.
57. Ibid., pp.9-14.
58. Ibid., p.29.
59. Ibid., p.50.
60. Ibid., p.107.
61. Ibid., p.111.
62. Ibid., p.196.
63. Brown, *Bury Heart*, p.439.
64. Miller, *Ghost Dance*, p.167.
65. Ibid., pp243-266.
66. Ibid., p.276.
67. Ibid., p.307.
68. Brown, *Bury Heart*, p.435.
69. Deloria, *Custer*, pp.106-112.
70. Fred Eggan, *The American Indian: Perspectives for the Study of Social Change* (Chicago: Aldine Publishing, 1966), p.144.
71. Ibid., p.145.
72. Deloria, *Custer*, p.17.
73. Ibid., pp.18-20.
74. Eggan, *American Indian*, p.165.
75. Ibid., p.166.

76. Paul R. Wieck, "From Wards to Freeman," *New Republic*, April 7, 1973, p.17.
77. Ibid.
78. Deloria, *Custer*, p.276.

V. American Indian Movement (AIM)

1. Vine Deloria, Jr., *Behind the Trail of Broken Treaties: A Declaration of Independence* (New York: Delacorte Press, 1974), p.4.
2. Ibid., p.25.
3. Ibid., 26.
4. Ibid., pp.26-28.
5. Ibid., p.29.
6. Ibid., p.32.
7. Ibid., pp.33-35.
8. "Aim: What's it all about?" *Akwesasne Notes*, published by the Mohawk Nation, Late 1973, p.15.
9. Deloria, *Behind Trail*, p.36.
10. "AIM: What's it all about?" p.15.
11. Ibid.
12. Tom Bates, "The Government's Secret War Against the Indian," *Oregon Times*, February/March 1976, p.19.
13. "AIM: What's it all about?" p.15.
14. Ibid.
15. Bates, "Secret War." P.19.
16. Deloria, *Behind Trail*, p.37.
17. Ibid.
18. Ibid., p.38.
19. Ibid., p.39-40.

20. Idem., "The Theological Dimension of the Indian Protest Movement," *Christian Century*, September 19, 1973, p.913.

21. Ibid.

22. Interview with John Spense, Scholar in Residence, White Cloud Center for the American Indian and Alaskan Native Health Research and Development, Portland, Oregon, October 8, 1976.

23. Frances Svensson, "Language as Ideology: The American Indian Case," *American Indian Culture and Research Journal*, University of California, Los Angeles, vol.1, no.3, (1975): p.34.

24. Deloria, *Behind Trail*, p.43.

25. Interview with Devere East Man, spiritual leader for Indians in Portland, Oregon, area, counselor for White Cloud Center, October 14, 1976.

26. Deloria, *Behind Trail*, p.43.

27. Ibid., p.43-44.

28. Ibid., p.45.

29. Ibid., p.46-52.

30. Hearings before Subcommittee to Investigate the Administration of the Internal Security Laws of the Committee on the Judiciary United States Senate, S. Doc. No. 71-508 (1976) p.91.

31. Deloria, *Behind Trail*, p.52.

32. Ibid., p.53.

33. *Akwesasne Notes*, January 1973, p.13.

34. Deloria, *Behind Trail*, p.54.

35. Summary of Hearings before Subcommittee to Investigate the Administration of the Internal Secu-

rity Laws of the Committee on the Judiciary, United States Senate, (1976) S. Doc. No. 76-598 O, p.10.

36. Deloria, "Theological dimension," p.913.
37. *Akwesasne Notes*, January 1973, p.13.
38. Jack Anderson, *The Anderson Papers* (New York: Random House, 1973), pp.175-77.
39. Ibid., p.180.
40. Ibid., pp.181-89.
41. Ibid., pp.190-92.
42. Ibid., p.193.

VI. Wounded Knee – 1973
1. Bates, "Secret War," p.17.
2. Deloria, *Behind Trail*, p.64.
3. Bates, "Secret War," p.17.
4. Deloria, *Behind Trail*, p.64.
5. Ibid., p.11.
6. William T. Hanlon, "Whose Ox Was Gored at Wounded Knee," *America*, March 16, 1974, p.191.
7. Deloria, *Behind Trail*, pp.70-71.
8. Wieck, "From Wards," p.17.
9. Ibid., p.16.
10. Bates, "Secret War," p.17.
11. Deloria, "Theological Dimension," p.913.
12. Ted Elbert, "Wounded Knee: A Struggle for Self-Determination," *Christian Century*, March 28, 1973, p.356.
13. Ibid., p.357.
14. Ibid.
15. Wieck, "From Wards," p.17.
16. Ibid.

17. Desmond Smith, "The Media Coup d'Etat," *Nation*, June 25, 1973, p.807.
18. Ibid., p.808.
19. Ibid.
20. Ibid., p.806.
21. "A Suspenseful Show of Red Power," *Time*, March 19, 1973, p.16.
22. Ibid.
23. Bates, "Secret War," p.17.
24. Ibid.
25. Ibid., p.18.
26. Ibid.
27. Russell Dilley, "Standoff at Wounded Knee," *Christian Century*, May 9, 1973, p.56.
28. Terri Schultz, "Bamboozle Me Not at Wounded Knee," *Harper's Magazine*, June 1973, p.56.
29. Ibid., p.46.
30. Ibid., p.55.
31. Ibid.
32. "Suspenseful Show," p.16.
33. Ibid.
34. Ibid.
35. Ibid.
36. Deloria, *Behind Trail*, pp.77-78.
37. Rita Keshena, "The role of American Indians in Motion Pictures," *American Indian Culture and Research Journal*, vol.1, no.2, (1974): p.28.
38. Smith, "Media Coup d'état," p.808.
39. Deloria, "Out of a Wounded Past," *Ramparts*, March 1975, p.29.
40. "Suspenseful Show," p.17.

41. "Trap at Wounded Knee," *Time*, March 26, 1973, p.67.
42. Ibid.
43. "Wounded Knee Fiasco," *National Review*, March 30, 1973, pp.352-53.
44. "Clean up Wounded Knee," *National Review*, April 13, 1973, pp.405-6.
45. "Pain in the Knee," *National Review*, May 11, 1973, p.512.
46. Ibid.
47. Schultz, "Bamboozle," p.56.
48. *world Book Year Book 1974*, "American Indian," p.354.
49. "Behind the Second Battle at Wounded Knee," *Time*, March 19, 1973, p.17.
50. "Media Coup d'état," p.808.
51. Ibid., 809.
52. Bates, "Secret War," p.18.
53. Deloria, "Theological Dimension," p.914.
54. *Akwesasne Notes*, Late 1973, p.12.

VII. Testimony of Douglass Durham, FBI Operative

1. John P. Adams, "AIM, the Church and the FBI: The Douglass Durham Case," *Christian Century*, May 14, 1975, p.489.
2. Hearing before Subcommittee Internal Security, p.11.
3. Rowe, *Press Freedoms*, pp.29-31.
4. Ibid, p.32.
5. Ibid.
6. Ibid., p.33.
7. Ibid.

8.   Adams, "AIM, Church," p.489.
9.   Ibid., p.489.
10. Ibid.
11. Ibid.
12. Ibid., p.490.
13. Ibid.
14. Ibid., p.490-91.
15. Ibid., p.491.
16. Hearing Subcommittee Internal Security, p.25.
17. Ibid., p.29.
18. Ibid., p.30.
19. Ibid., p.33.
20. Ibid., p.34.
21. Ibid., p.36.
22. Adams, "AIM, Church," p.492.
23. Summary of Hearings Internal Security, p.70.
24. Hearings Subcommittee Internal Security, p.70.
25. Ibid., pp.163-64.
26. Adams, "AIM, Church," p.492.
27. "Panel Concludes AIM goals bad for Indian Image," *Oregonian*, Sunrise Edition, September 20, 1976, p.1.
28. "Indian Movement Assails Senate Report," *Oregon Journal*, September 21, 1976, pt.3, p.24.
29. "Local Indian Leaders Laud AIM's Role," *Oregonian*, September 20, 1976.
30. Ibid.
31. Ibid.
32. Adams, "AIM, Church," p.494.
33. Ibid.
34. Ibid.

VIII. Dennis Banks in Oregon

1. "Pine Ridge Shootout," *Time*, July 7, 1975, p.8.
2. Bates, "Secret War," p.18.
3. Ibid., p.18.
4. "Danger seen for AIM Chief," *Oregon Journal*, September 15, 1976, pt.3, p.12.
5. "AIM activist sentenced," *Oregonian*, June 3, 1977, 3M, p.A13.
6. Bates, "Secret War," p.18.
7. K.M. Hawkins, "Means charges FBI 'set up' shooting," *Vanguard*, Portland State University, Oregon, May 11, 1976, p.1.
8. Ibid.
9. "Jury acquits AIM leader of murder," *Oregonian*, August 7, 1976, p.1.
10. Wayne Thompson, "Banks trial may make Portland AIM's big target," *Sunday Oregonian*, Forum, April 18, 1976, sec. C, p.1.
11. Ibid.
12. "Dennis Banks' wife placed on probation," *Oregon Journal*, September 13, 1976, p.2.
13. Bates, "Secret War," p.15.
14. Jim Hill, "On firearms charges – Banks' wife gets 3 years probation," *Oregonian*, September 14, 1976, 4M, p.B1.
15. Thompson, "Portland AIM's target," p.2M, C1.
16. Quinton Smith, "Banks Seeks Oregon Sanctuary," *Oregon Journal*, April 23, 1976, p. (3) 8.
17. "Prosecution delay bid rejected in AIM trial," *Oregonian*, April 28, 1976, p.1.

18. "Methodists Hear Banks' Flee Story," *Oregon Journal*, May 4, 1976.

19. "Dismissal Seen in Banks Charge," *Oregon Journal*, May 4, 1976, p. (3) 2.

20. "Indians plead for end to injustice," *Sunday Oregonian*, May 9, 1976, pt. C, p.6.

21. Janet Christ, "Delay in Banks Trial Sought," *Oregon Journal*, May 11, 1976, p.4M, A15.

22. Jim Hill, "Lezak denies claim that Banks trial stalled," *Oregonian*, May 12, 1976, p.C 8.

23. "U.S. Still Hopes to Try Banks on Explosive Rap," *Oregon Journal*, May 12, 1976, p.1.

24. Robert Olmos, "Banks expects reindictment," *Oregonian*, May 13, 1976, p.4M, A15.

25. "Judge sets Banks' bail at $10,000," *Oregon Journal*, May 13, 1976, p.1.

26. "U.S. Still Hopes to Try Banks on Explosive Rap," *Oregon Journal*, May 13, 1976, p.2.

27. "Straub Asks Banks Defense," *Oregon Journal*, May 18, 1976, p. (3) 2.

28. "Banks Beyond His Control, Straub Says," *Oregon Journal*, June 9, 1976, p.1.

29. Ed Mosey, "Banks in California – Straub drops AIM extradition case," *Oregonian*, June 10, 1976, p.1.

30. "Judge grants Straub delay on Banks" *Oregonian*, June 16, 1976, sec. D, p. 4M 1.

31. Janet Christ, "Banks wins 30-day delay," *Oregon Journal*, June 15, 1976, p. (3) 2.

32. "Banks out on bond," *Oregonian*, June 17, 1976.

33. "New Banks date Sought," *Oregon Journal*, June 17, 1976, p.2.

Marilyn Catherine McDonald MA

34. Janet Christ, "Straub Extradition Decision Promised," *Oregon Journal*, June 22, 1976, p.2.
35. Steven Carter, "Banks complaint dismissed: warrant ordered," *Oregonian*, July 3, 1976, p.1.
36. "Hearing for Banks Postponed," *Oregon Journal*, September 16, 1976, p.1.
37. "S.D. wins court test for Banks," *Oregonian*, April 26, 1976, p. A12, 3M.
38. Telephone conversation with officer in the U.S. Marshal's office in Portland, Oregon, Federal Courthouse building.

Conclusion

1. Neal R. Pierce, "Reservation-area whites bear load for earlier mistreatment of Indians," *Oregonian*, September 13, 1976, sec. B, p.7.
2. "Watchdog bites if press strays from truth, former Rep. Green reports," *Oregonian*, July 7, 1977, sec. A, p.15.

ALERT THE MEDIA SOURCES CONSULTED

Books

Anderson, Jack. *The Anderson Papers*. New York: Random House, 1973.

Brown, Dee. *Bury My Heart at Wounded Knee*. New York: Holt, Rinehart and Winston, 1970.

Burke, Kenneth. *Language as Symbolic Action*. Los Angeles: University of California Press, 1966.

Castaneda, Carlos. *Journey to Ixtlan*. New York: Pocket Books, 1975.

Dennis, Everette E., and Rivers, William L. *Other Voices: The New Journalism in America*, San Francisco: Canfield Press, 1974.

Marilyn Catherine McDonald MA

Deloria, Vine, Jr. *We Speak, You Listen.* New York: Mac-Millan Publishing Co., 1970.

_____. *Custer Died for Your Sins.* New York: MacMillan Publishing Co., 1969.

_____. *Behind the Trail of Broken Treaties: A Declaration of Independence.* New York: Delacorte Press, 1974.

Eggan, Fred. *The American Indian: Perspectives for the Study of Social Change.* Chicago: Aldine Publishing, 1966.

Gamson, William A. *Power and Discontent.* Illinois: The Dorsey Press, 1968.

Gelb, Joyce, and Palley, Marian Lief. *The Politics of Social Change.* New York: Holt, Rinehart and Winston, 1971.

Griffin, Leland M. " A Dramatistic Theory of the Rhetoric of Movements," in *Critical Responses to Kenneth Burke,* Edited by William H. Rueckert. Minnesota: University of Minnesota Press, 1969.

Grimshaw, Allen D. *Racial Violence in the United States.* Chicago: Aldine Publishing Co., 1969.

Hall, Edward T., Ph.D. *The Silent Language.* Connecticut: Fawcett Publications, 1959.

Hassick, Royal B. *The Sioux: Life and Customs of a Warrior Society.* Norman: University of Oklahoma Press, 1964.

Innis, Harold A. *The Bias of Communication.* Toronto: University of Toronto Press, 1951.

Lindesmith, Alfred R., and Strauss, Anselm L. *social Psychology.* New York: Holt, Rinehart and Winston, 1969.

McLuhan, Marshall. *The Medium is the Massage.* United States and Canada: Bantam Books, Inc., 1967.

Miller, David Humphreys. *Ghost Dance.* New York: Duell, Sloan and Pierce, 1959..

Neihardt, John G. *Black Elk Speaks.* New York: Willaim Morrow and Co., 1932.

Schlesinger, Arthur M. *Prelude to Independence: The Newspaper War on Britain 1964-1776.* New York: Alfred A. Knopf, 1958.

Sidran, Ben. *Black Talk.* New York: Harper Row Publishing Co., paperback, 1971.

Seiden, Martin H. *Who Controls the Mass Media? Popular Myths and Economic Realities.* New York: Basic Books, Inc., 1974.

Servan-Schreiber, Jean-Louis. *The Power to Inform, Media: The business of information.* New York: McGraw-Hill, 1974.

Shibutani, Tamotsu. *Improvised News.* New York: Bobbs-Merrill Co., 1966.

Marilyn Catherine McDonald MA

Skolnick, Jerome. *The Politics of Protest, Violent Aspects of Protest and Confrontation.* Staff report to the National Commission on Causes and Prevention of Violence. New York: Simon and Schuster, 1969.

Smelser, Neil J. *Theory of Collective Behavior.* New York: The Free Press of Glencoe, 1963.

Stein, Robert. *Media Power: Who is Shaping your Picture of the World?* Boston: Houghton Mifflin, 1972.

Storm, Hyemeyohsts. *Seven Arrows.* New York: Harper Row, 1972.

Published Reports

Report of the Twentieth Century Fund Task Force on the Government and the Press. Press Freedoms Under Pressure. James Rowe, Chairman. Backgrund paper by Fred P. Graham. New York:, Twentieth Century Fund, 1972.

Hearings before the Subcommittee to Investigate the Administration of the Internal Security Laws of the Committee on the Judiciary of the United States Senate. Revolutionary Activities Within the United States. The American Indian Movement. By James O. Eastland, Chairman. Testimony of Douglass Frank Durham, taken in executive session on 6 April 1976. S.Doc. No. 71-508. Washington, D.C.: Government Printing Office, 1976.

Summary of Hearings before the Subcommittee to Investigate Administration of the Internal Security Laws of the Committee on the Judiciary of the United States Senate. Revolutionary Activities Within the United States. The American Indian Movement. By James O. Eastland, Chairman. S. Doc. No. 76-598 0. Washington, D.C.: Government Printing Office, 1976.

Articles in Journals or Magazines

Journals

Good Tracks, Jimm G. "Native American Noninterference," *Social Work* (November 1973): 30-34.

Keshena, Rita. "The Role of American Indians in Motion Pictures," *American Indian Culture and Research Journal* – 1 no.2 (1974)

Marx, Gary T., and Wood, James L. "Strands of Theory and Research in Collective Behavior," *Annual Review of Sociology* – 1 (1975) p. 363-428.

Svensson, Frances. "Language as Ideology: The American Indian Case," *American Indian Culture and Research Journal* – 1 no.3 (1975).

Magazines

Adams, John P. "AIM, the Church and the FBI: The Douglass Durham Case," *Christian Century*, May 14, 1975, pp.489-95.

Marilyn Catherine McDonald MA

Bates, Tom. "The Government's Secret War Against the Indian," *Oregon Times*, February/March 1976, pp.14-19.

Deloria, Vine, Jr. "The Theological Dimension of the Indian Protest Movement," *Christian Century*, September 19, 1973, pp.912-14.

_____. "Religion and the Modern American Indian," *Current History*, December 1974, pp.28-32.

_____. "The Indian Movement: Out of a Wounded Past," *Ramparts*, March 1975, pp.28-32.

Dilley, Russell. "Standoff at Wounded Knee," *Christian Century*, May 9, 1973, pp.527-8.

Elbert, Ted. "Wounded Knee: A Struggle for Self-Determination," *Christian Century*, March 28, 1973, pp.356-7.
Hanlon, William T. "Whose Ox Was Gored at Wounded Knee," *America*, March 16, 1974, pp.190-4.

Schultz, Terri. "Bamboozle Me Not at Wounded Knee," *Harper's Magazine*, June 1973, pp.46-56.

Smith, Desmond. "The Media Coup d'état," *Nation*, June 25, 1973, pp.806-9.

Wieck, Paul R. "From Wards to Freeman," *New Republic*, April 7, 1973, pp.16-19.

Magazine Articles (unsigned)

National Review

"Wounded Knee Fiasco," March 30, 1973, pp.352-3.

"Pain in the Knee," May 11, 1073, p.512.

"Clean up Wounded Knee," April 13, 1973.

Press Woman

"Television news 'new kid on the block,'" Publication of the National Federation of Press Women, Inc., November 1976, p.2.

Time

"Suspenseful Show of Red Power," March 19, 1973, pp.16-18.

"Behind the Second Battle of Wounded Knee," March 19, 1973, p.17.

"Trap at Wounded Knee," March 26, 1973, p.67.

"Pine Ridge Shootout," July 7, 1975, p.8.

Articles in Encyclopedia's Yearbooks

Marilyn Catherine McDonald MA

The World Book Year Book 1975, "From Triumph to Tragedy," Peter Lisagor, pp.58-79.

The World Book Year Book 1974. "American Indian," p.354.

Newspapers

Akwesasne Notes, published by the Mohawk Nation, January 1973, and Late 1973.

Oregonian (Portland)

"Disclosure by TV Newsmen urged," Leverett Richards, October 27, 1976, sec. C, p.8.

"Panel Concludes AIM goals bad for Indian Image," September 20, 1976, p.1.

"Local Indian Leaders laud AIM's role," September 20, 1976, p.1.

"AIM activist sentenced," June 3, 1977, sec.A, p.13.

"Jury acquits AIM leader of murder," August 7, 1976, p.1.

"Banks' wife gets 3 years probation," Jim Hill, September 14, 1976, sec.B, p.1.

"Prosecution delay bid rejected in AIM trial," April 28, 1976, p.1.

"Indians plead for end to injustices," May 9, 1976, sec.C, p.6.

"Lezak denies claim that Banks trial stalled," Jim Hill, May 12, 1976, sec.C, p.8.

"Banks expects reindictment," Robert Olmos, May 13, 1976, sec.A, p.16.

"Judge grants Straub delay on Banks," June 16, 1976, sec.D, p.1.

"Banks out on bond," June 17, 1976, sec.B, p.3.

"Watchdog bites if press strays from truth," July 7, 1977, p.15.

"Banks complaint dismissed; warrant ordered," Steven Carter, July 3, 1976, p.1.

"S.D. wins court test for Banks," April 26, 1976, sec.A, p.12.

"Reservation-area whites bear load for earlier mistreatment of Indians," Neal R. Pierce, September 13, 1976, sec.B, p.7.

Oregon Journal (Portland)

"Indian Movement Assails Senate Report," September 21, 1976, p.24.

"Danger seen for AIM Chief," September 15, 1976, p.12.

Marilyn Catherine McDonald MA

"Dennis Banks' wife placed on probation," September 13, 1976, p.2.
"Banks Seeks Oregon Sanctuary," Quinton Smith, April 23, 1976, p.8.

"Methodists Hear Banks' Flee Story," May 4, 1976.

"Dismissal Seen in Banks Charge," May 4, 1976, p.2.

"Delay in Banks Trial Sought," Janet Christ, May 11, 1976, p.3.

"U.S. Still Hopes to Try Banks on Explosive Rap," May 13, p.2.

"Straub Asks Banks Defense," May 18, 1976, p.2.

"Banks Beyond His Control, Straub says," June 9, 1976, p.1.

"Banks Wins 30-day delay," June 15, 1976, p.2.

"New Banks date sought," June 17, 1976, p.2.

"Straub Extradition Decision Promised," Janet Christ, June 22, 1976, p.2.

"Hearing for Banks Postponed," September 16, 1976, p.1.

Vanguard (Portland State University, Oregon)

"Means charges FBI 'set up' shooting," K.M. Hawkins, May 11, 1976.

Interviews

East Man, Devere "Papasan." Indian spiritual leader and counselor, Portland, Oregon, October 14, 1976.

Spense, John. Scholar in Residence, White Cloud Center, Portland, Oregon, October 8, 1976.

U.S. Marshals office, (representative) Portland, Oregon, May 10, 1976.

EPILOGUE

Advertising and public relations professionals, as well as politicians, businesses and public service organizations live or die based on their ability or inability to "alert the media" – an old expression for getting the message to the masses – the public. Getting people to buy your product or empathize with you and your issues.

Today's media consumer barely, and rarely, consumes hard news. The two-minute television or other electronic media sound bites are here today and gone tomorrow – or within the hour. The newer and younger generation prefers the smaller computer screens for surfing the web, or blogging, for information, rather than the "media alerts, breaking news or just-in" reports or the scoops on the major alphabet networks, as well as satellite or cable news channels.

Television, primarily, is for watching the sporting events of the major professional teams and leagues or the college sports, as well as the current sit-com, made-for-television series, reality show or pay-for-view movies: getting their satirical laughs and semi-news from *Saturday Night Live*, *The Daily Show* and the *Colbert Report*.

A large number of the books currently being published are written by former high-ranking government officials, about them, or those political campaigners who want-to-be. One wonders how many of the non-fiction books bought are actually being read.

According to a *Publishers Weekly* report the number of hours spent reading books, per person, declined from 101 in 1995 to 86 in 2004. During that same period the number of hours spent watching television increased from 1,580 to 1,673.

Because of the shift in how most people perceive and receive their news, issue oriented political movements increasingly are pushed to the background in favor of the government's administrative and congressional issues, agendas or "talking points." Thus, issues such as those posed by the American Indian Movement (AIM), which once commanded attention from newspapers, magazines and television have taken second place with the mass media. Their issues have given way to the activities surrounding the current President, current military and security issues, natural disasters, crimes, missing persons, current scandals and corruption.

Following their 1973 "occupation" of Wounded Knee in South Dakota, members of the American Indian Movement (AIM) slipped into relative media obscurity, while facing several rounds of court battles for subsequent decades. AIM members' original intent for the "occupation" and events leading up to that episode was lost on the American public. AIM activist Leonard Peltier still remains in prison. Casino funds continue to be exploited by those businesses pretending to help. And, the voices of the people betrayed by the U.S. Government's broken treaties still echo through the Black Hills of South Dakota's wilderness and fields once rich with gold, minerals and uranium.

References to the American Indian have become the "Native American," but little else has changed in recognizing their claims for justice in the courts. The Native American demand for media attention no longer can be heard over the public demand to know why the government has taken our men and women to fight for freedom for the citizens of other countries. The public wants to know why we spend hundreds of billions of taxpayers' dollars to repair the damages we caused; and spends billions to raise the standard of living of Middle East countries – to the neglect of the children, elderly and underprivileged population of America.

Alerting the media through press releases, court action or public displays of outrage and indignation no longer serve the Native American cause. Although efforts and issues of AIM continue, they cannot crack the barrier with print or electronic media for the fleeting two-minute sound bite – let alone any in-depth or on-going coverage of their current concerns.

The Native American is not alone in an attempt to alert the media to its causes. Every other ethnic or religious group takes a back seat to the political cesspool of security leaks and unnamed sources in any administration's attempt at having its own way with the mass media – while, at the same time, claiming the media is "doing them wrong."

President Nixon began his attack by crying foul against the media coverage of his administration. He claimed, in effect, after he left office in disgrace following the Watergate scandal, that the press wouldn't have him to kick around anymore.

Nothing has changed. Subsequent administrations work the media for their own purposes, while claiming reporters are out to get them. The mass media, primarily network and cable television news have been the targets and pawns of politicians and the public, as have talk radio commentators and major publications such as *Time Magazine, the Washington Post* and the *New York Times.*

Good and bad reporting and unethical practices by the press and electronic media may exist, but destroying what we have will only make matters worse – and the American public is at risk of losing it's most cherished and important freedom – the watchdogs who guard our First Amendment rights to a press and information free of government control and interference.

My research continues to look for answers to questions about what happened to the American Indian Movement (AIM) and what happened to the mass media, and the effects of the rapidly changing modern technology brought to us through the Internet.

The matrix developed for my original work served me well in showing how the mass media came together with, and covered, a particular mass movement. I presented a picture of how we received information during a phase of AIM's development, and their protest finale at Wounded Knee.

Further research examines the relationship between AIM, the organization and the Native American cultural progression. Have these apparent divisions realigned themselves and repositioned themselves in the rapidly changing technological world of mass media coverage. Additional research attempts to answer for myself, and perhaps the public, some of the following general questions:

- What did American Indian Movement (AIM) leaders learn from their activism and protest period and how have they changed and/or adapted to the new technology and methods of gaining support and attracting attention through the media?

- What has happened to the way mass media (radio, television, print publications and Internet) cover and report events of national political or social interest?

- Generally, is the "free press" living up to its commitment to inform the public, or are media representatives becoming part of the news and/ or manipulating and "spinning" information?

Other questions, such as the following, will be addressed more specifically in the event I write a follow-up to *Alert the Media*.

Return of Indian Land

- Did the U.S. Government eventually do the right thing; returning land to the Indians? If so, when did it happen?

- What organizational, administrative, and cultural problems did the Native Americans on the reservations encounter as a result of the return of their land and sovereignty? How are they affected by tribal law and U.S. government and local laws?

- What changes occurred among the Sioux Indians, the main focus of *Alert the Media* and the formation of AIM?
- What brought about the $100 billion class action law suit by Native Americans against the United States Federal Government?

Return of Money – Casinos

- Are the Indians getting their revenge for all the broken treaties, broken promises, and destruction of their culture by learning the ways of the white man and taking back what they feel entitled to?
- How are the reservations that make money from the casinos doing with their new financial resources?
- Have Native Americans and their casino operations fallen into the hands of unscrupulous money and power handlers? Who is Jack Abramoff?

Sharing Culture

- How, when and where did the popularity of Indian culture and spirituality gain the interest of the new-age, counter-culture, and/or general population?
- Is there a true sharing of cultures underway in America?
- How is the "Indian Problem" viewed today?
- Does the public have a clue about "today's" Indian, or is the public still skeptical and resentful

regarding the land transfers, casino privileges, and radical protests of the Sixties and Seventies?

American Indian Movement (AIM) Survives

- How effective are AIM's website, speakers' bureau, radio station and public relations activities in reaching their own people and the general public?
- Does AIM have a clear sense of its vision, its mission?
- What are AIM's objectives, strategies, and methods?
- Who are their leaders? Who are their supporters and followers?

New Direction for Media

- What kinds of stories does the mass media tell us about the Indians these days? Is it mostly about such things as removing the Indian symbols or mascots from professional and college sports teams? Stopping the Atlanta Braves from using the tomahawk-chop hand gestures at ball games? Reporting that casinos avoid paying their fair share of a particular state's tax support?
- Has conglomeration of internet provider services, wire services, satellite radio, network and cable television, newspapers and magazines provided the public with real news or with controlled or slanted information. Or both?

- Are network television station owners and producers re-assessing themselves in light of the loss of several prominent news broadcasters?
- Who is watching the watchdog?

Political Issues and Media as News

- Three days, or less, of intense news coverage on major world, national or local news events – and then it's gone? Are these the days of the television "sound-bite?" Where does yesterday's news go? And why so soon? What is the nature of news, today? Are we moving that fast? Or, does the public have a short attention span?
- How can the average consumer of news discern importance or truth based on what they currently see, hear or read coming out of independent and conglomerate sources of information?
- What impact does the "unnamed source" have on reporting?
- Have government institutions and administrations become immune to the affects of political protest movements? Do they just spin their way out of everything?

AIM and other mass movements have discovered there is little or no progress through violence, and they search for more realistic ways to "alert the media" to their causes and concerns. What have we learned from their past to make us better reporters and consumers of news and other important information?

Marilyn Catherine McDonald, MA

Marilyn McDonald (Smith), a professional writer since 1967, published two books in her 70th year – *Little Girl Lost: a True Story of Tragic Death* and *Mother of Eight Survives Population Explosion: Just Between Us Column Selections.*

She earned her BS from Portland State University in 1975 and an MA in Communications from the University of Portland in 1977. Then, as a single parent she returned to the work force for the first time in 25 years. She climbed the corporate ladder in hospital public relations and publication production, owned an advertising agency, and served as an officer in several professional organizations. In addition, she volunteered as a suicide/crisis hotline counselor, a Court Appointed Special Advocate (CASA) for abused and neglected children, and a recovery counselor to women in prison.

With hundreds of newspaper and magazine feature stories to her credit, she now writes books and travel articles. Marilyn and her retired Air Force husband Harry Taylor are world travelers. They're at home in Central Oregon for the summers and spend their winters along the

Marilyn Catherine McDonald MA

Sea of Cortez in San Felipe, Baja, Mexico. As members of Rotary International, they support worldwide educational and charitable projects.